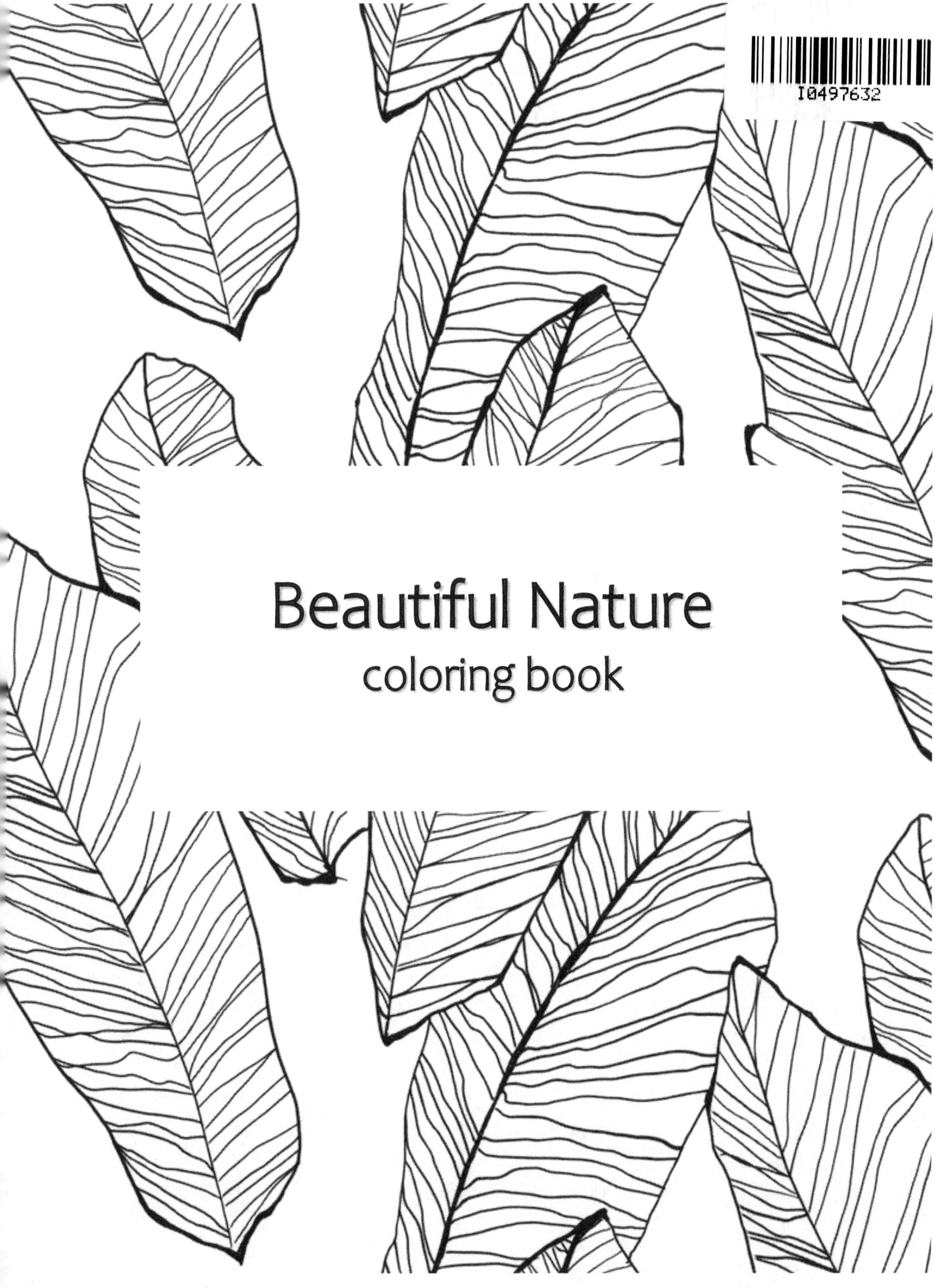

Beautiful Nature

coloring book

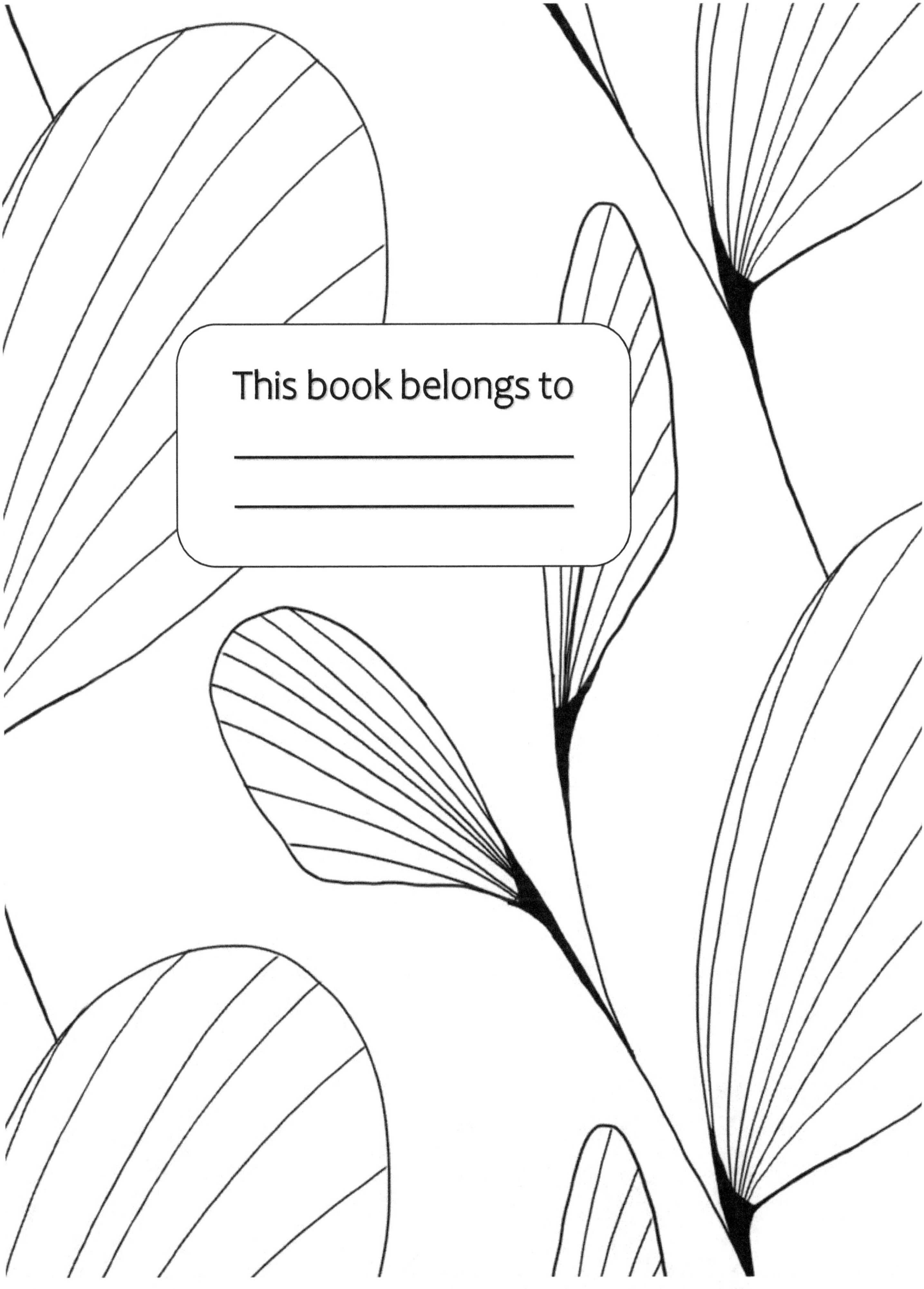

This book belongs to

____

____

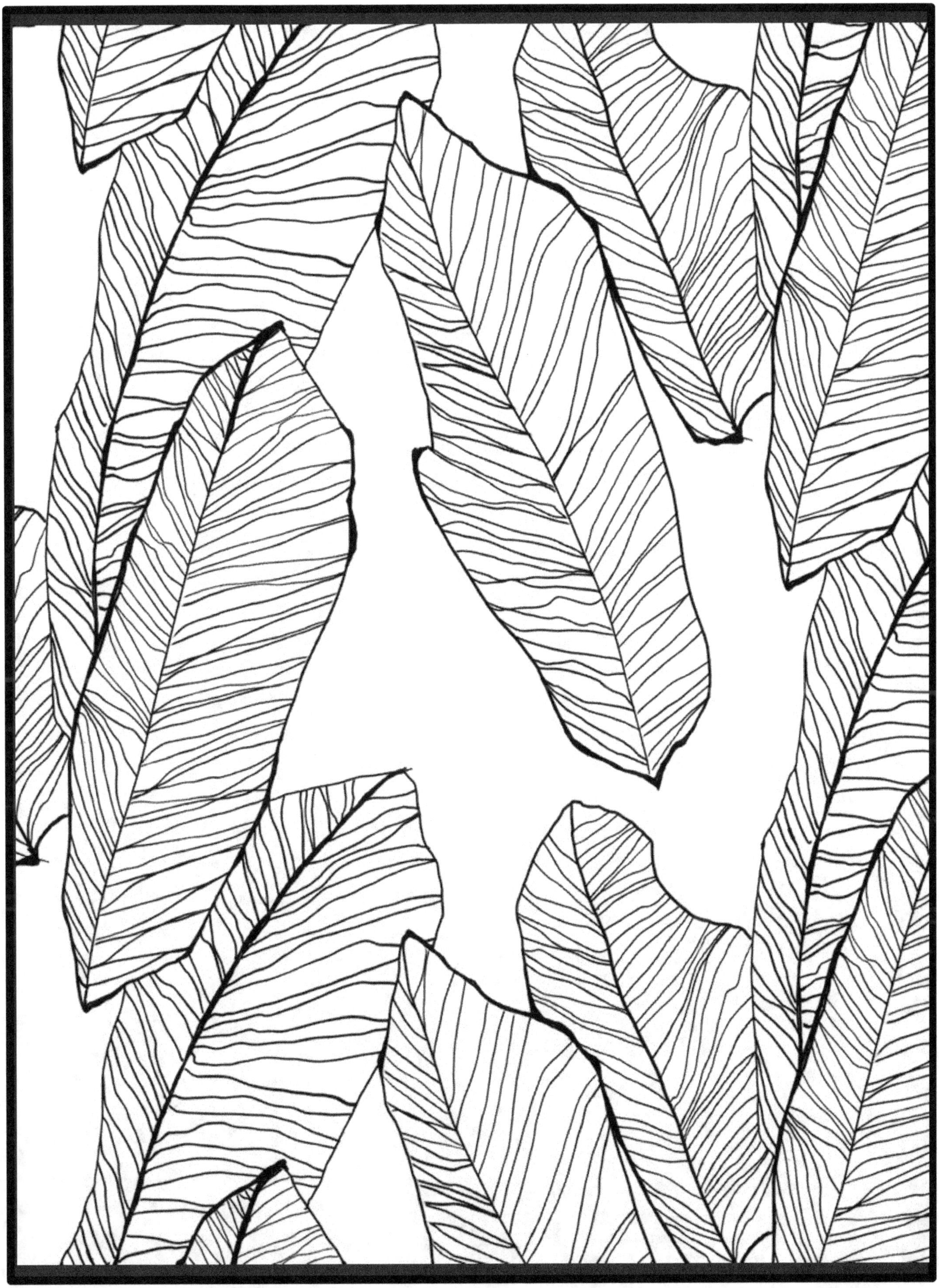

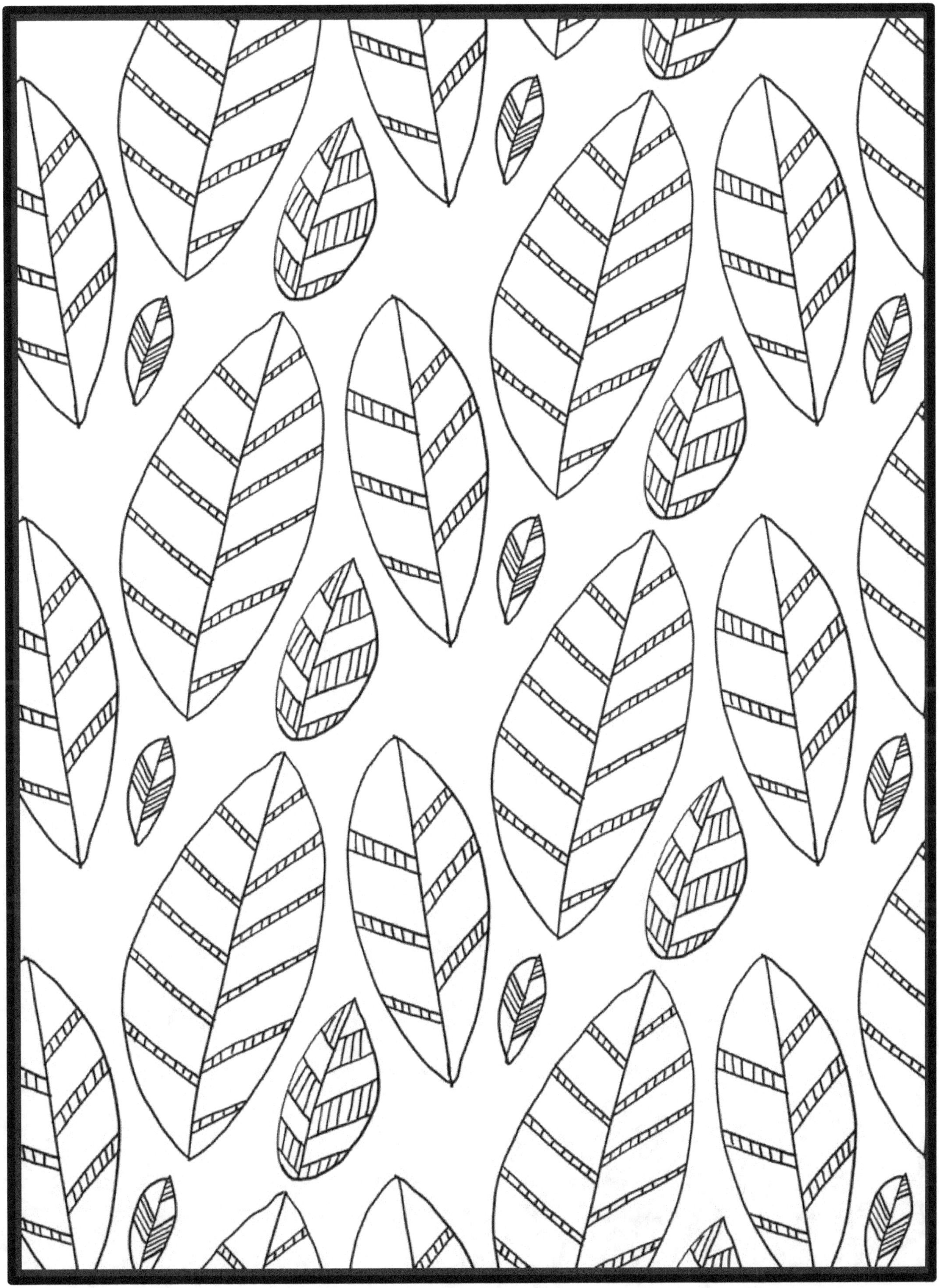

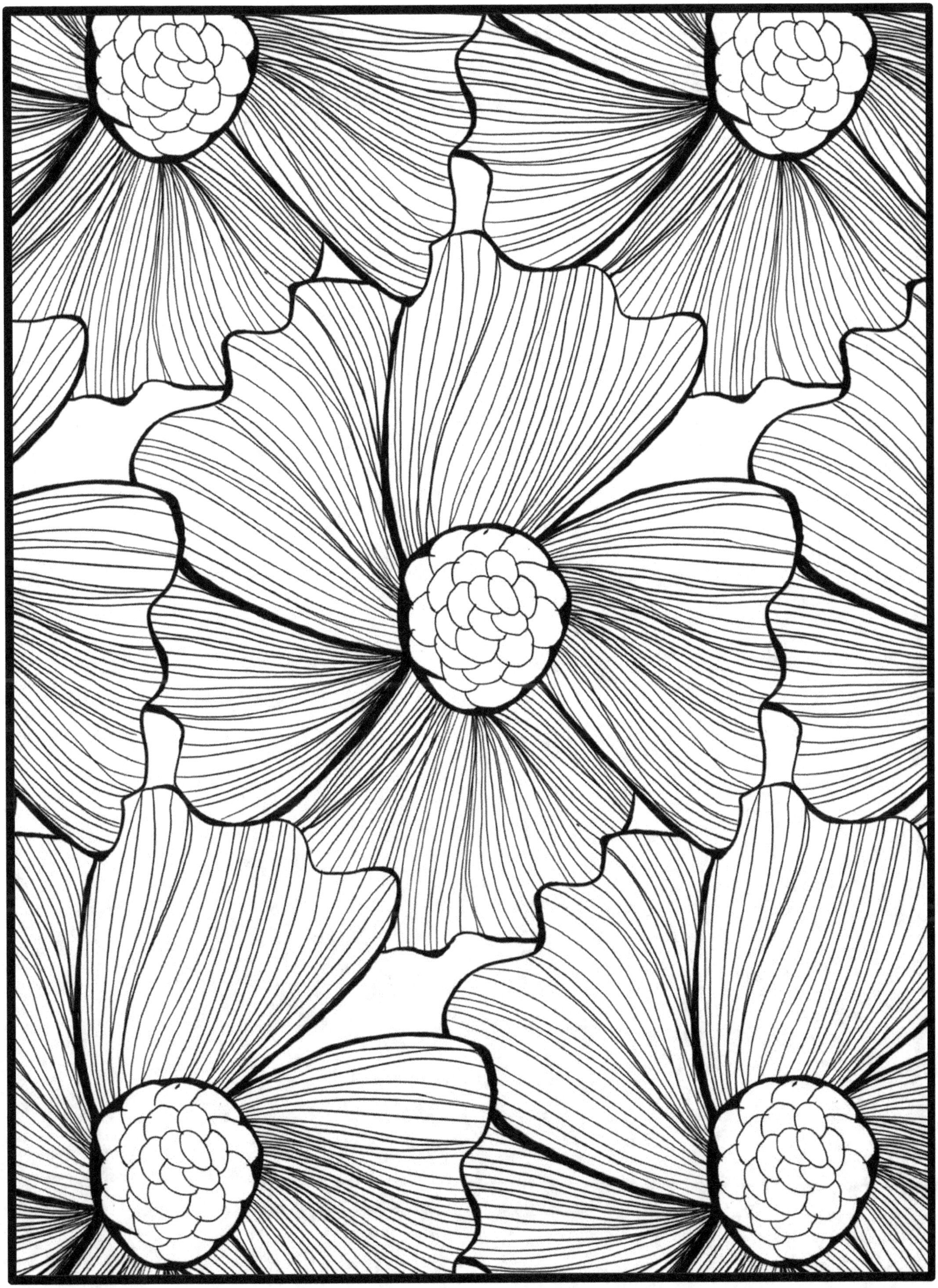

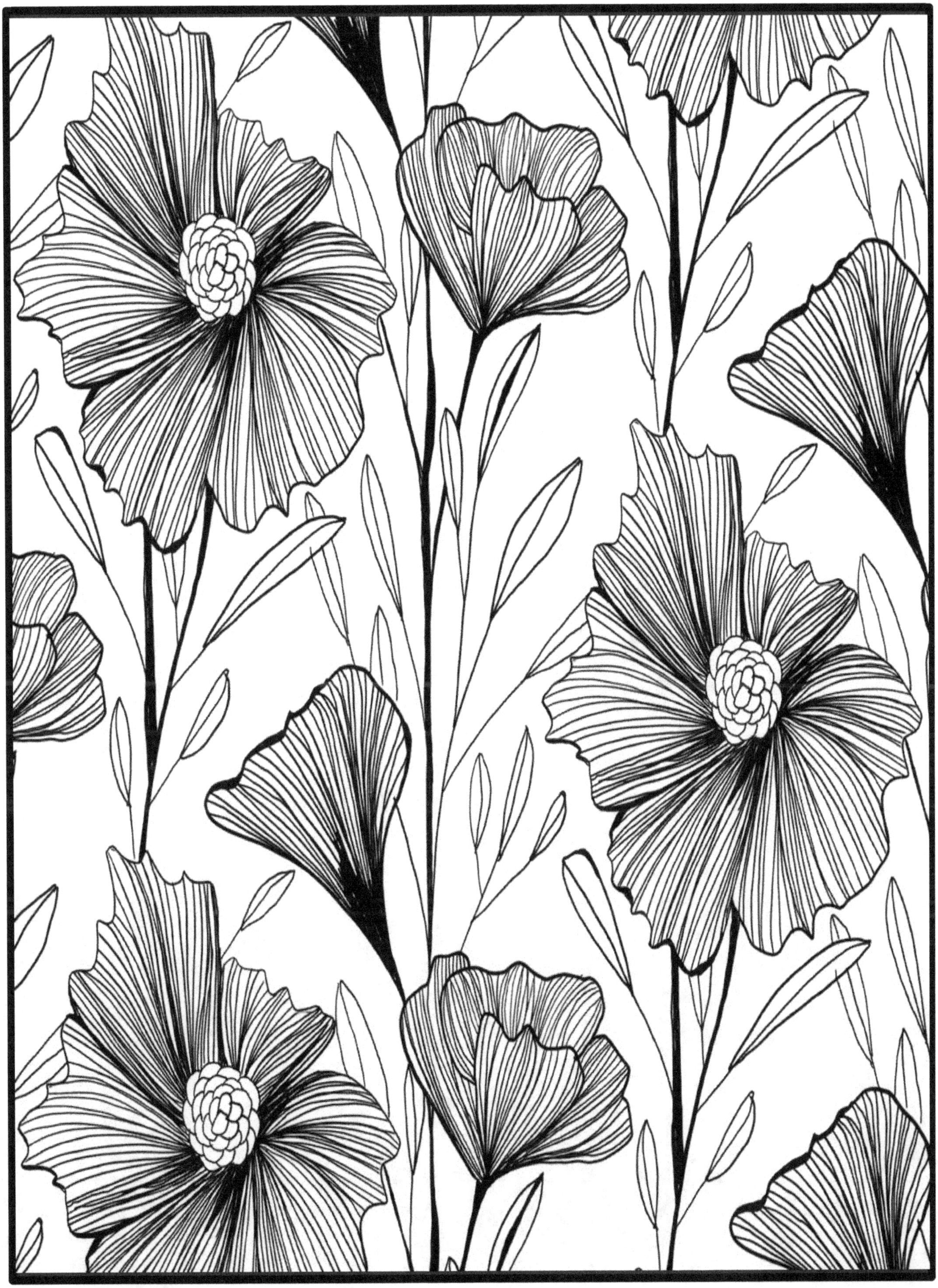

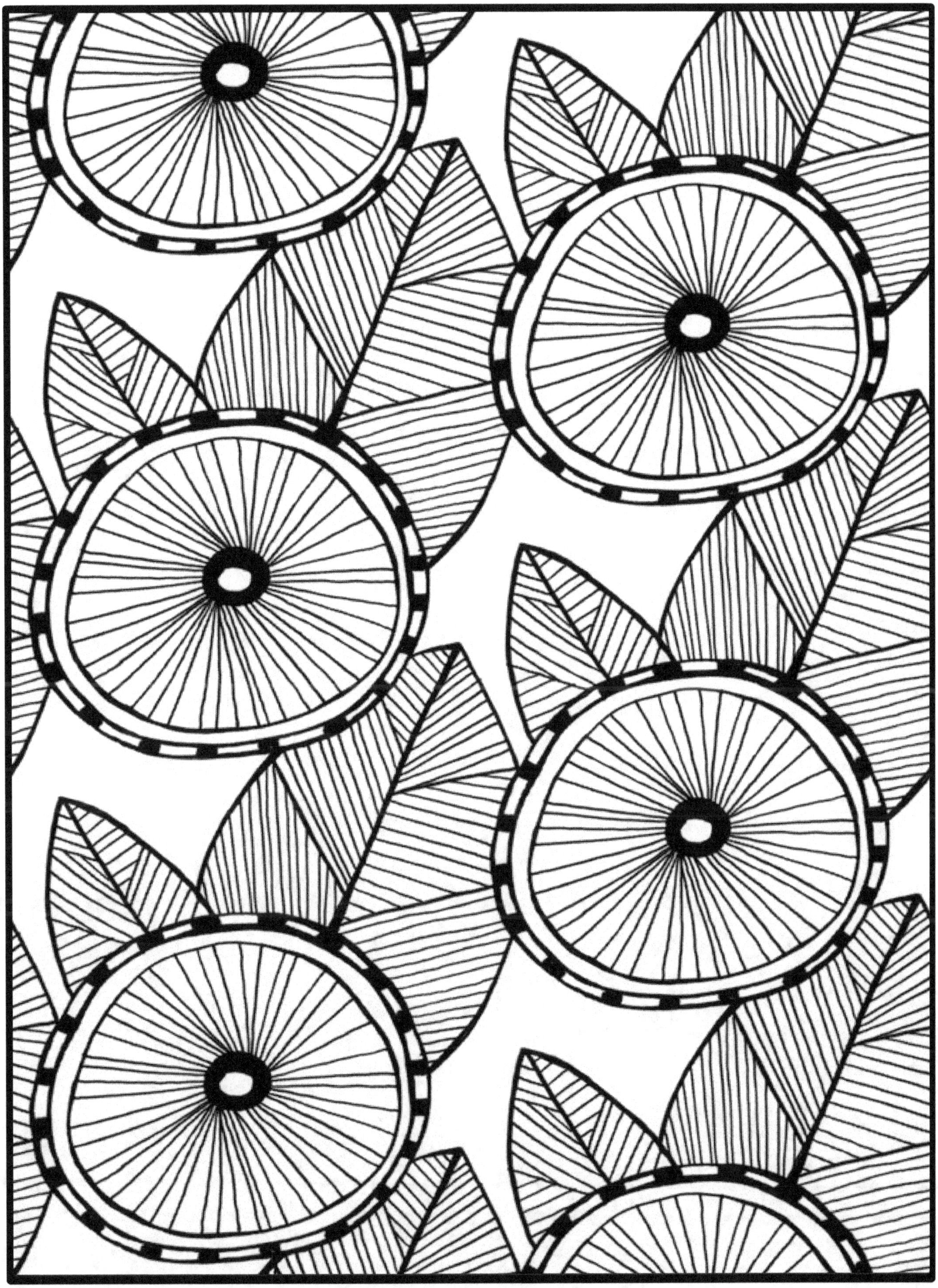

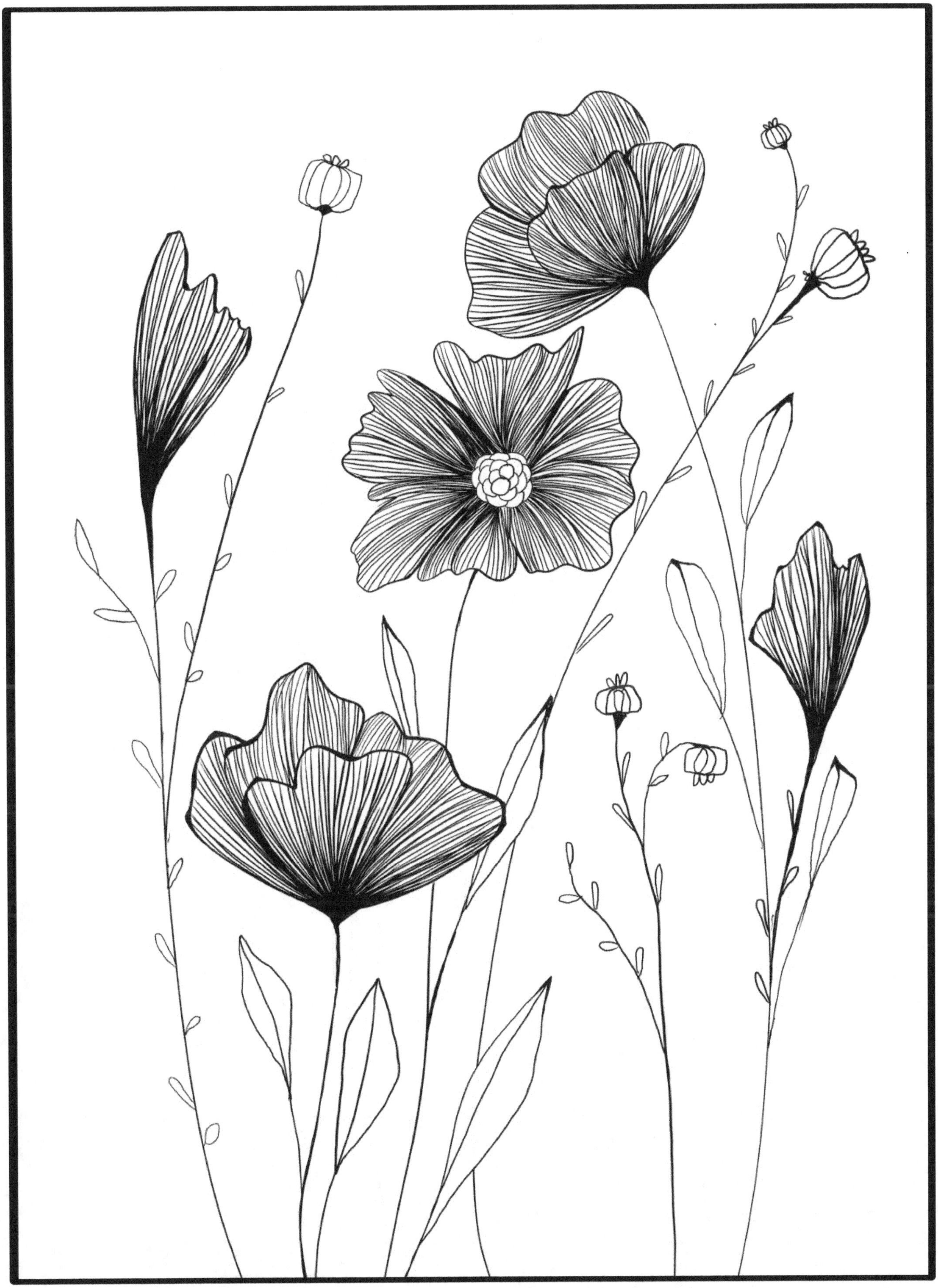

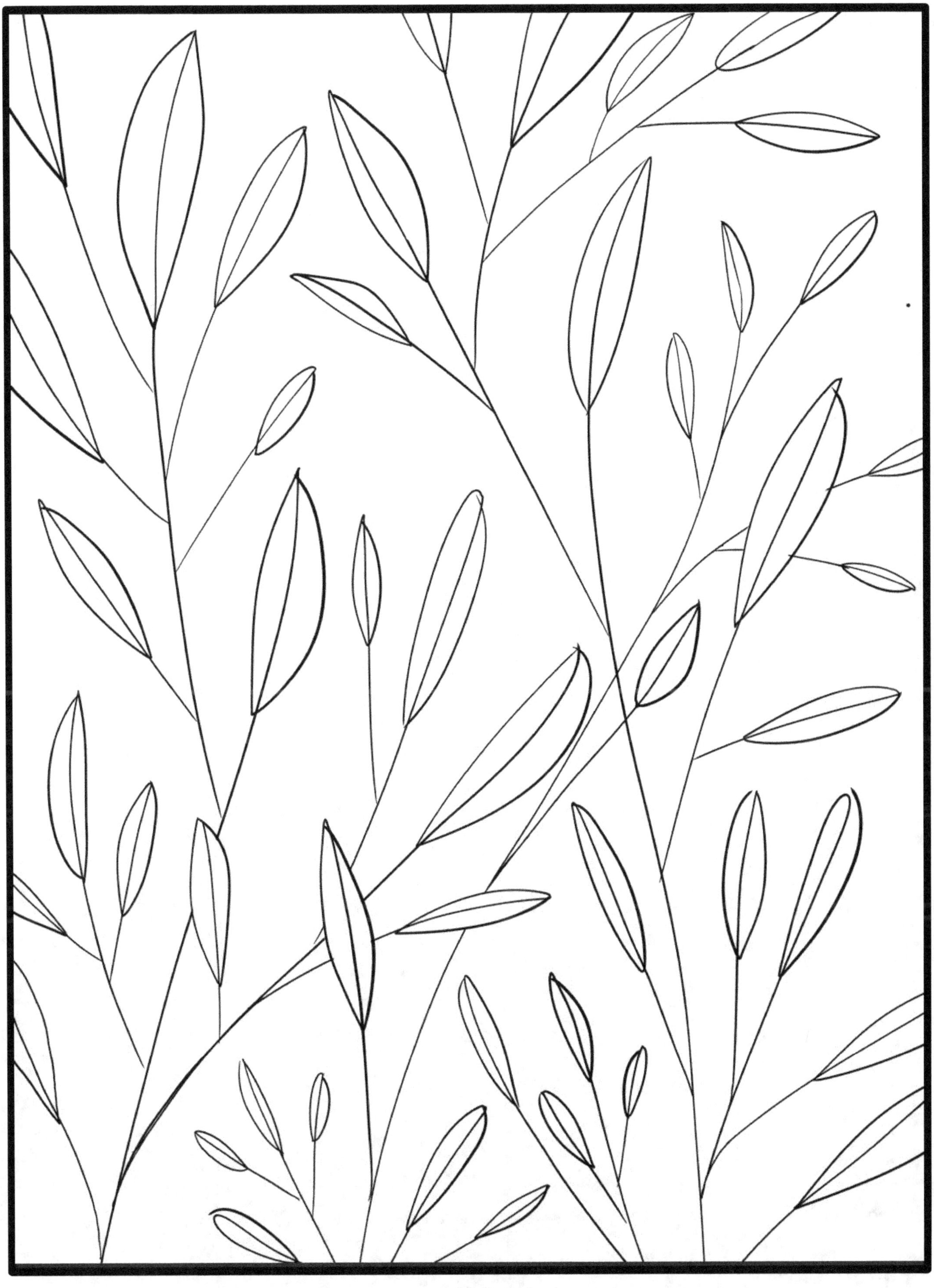

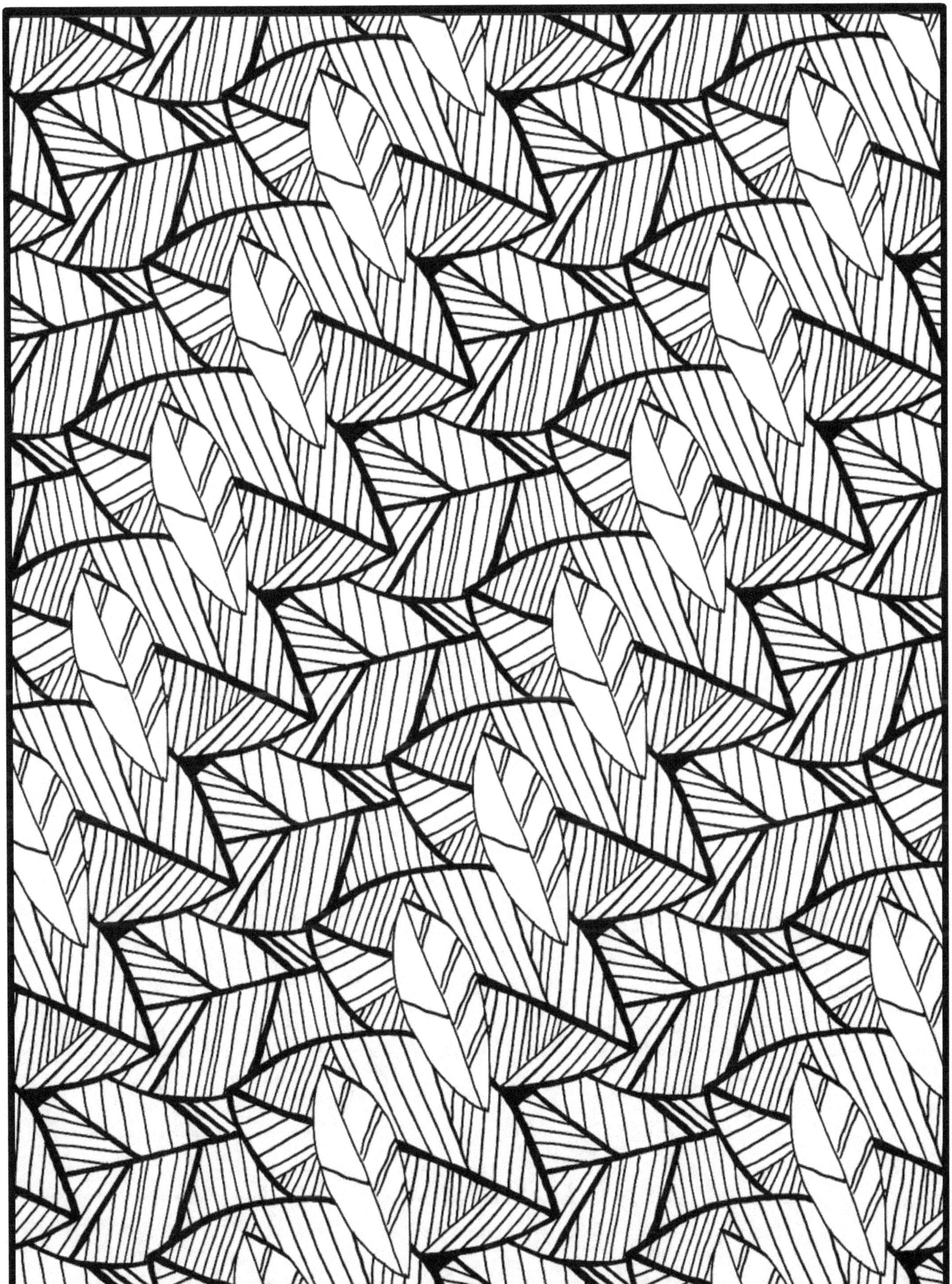

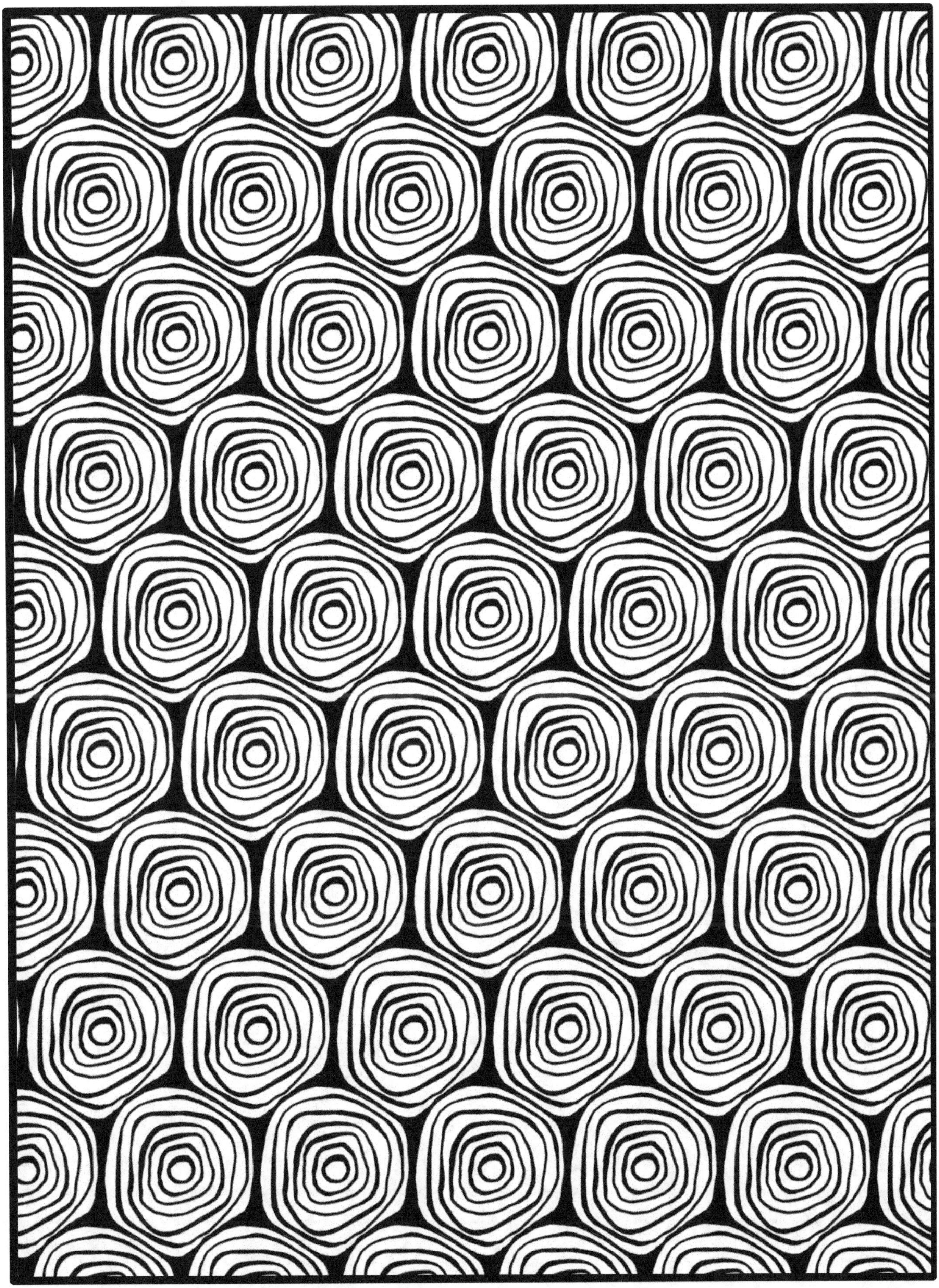

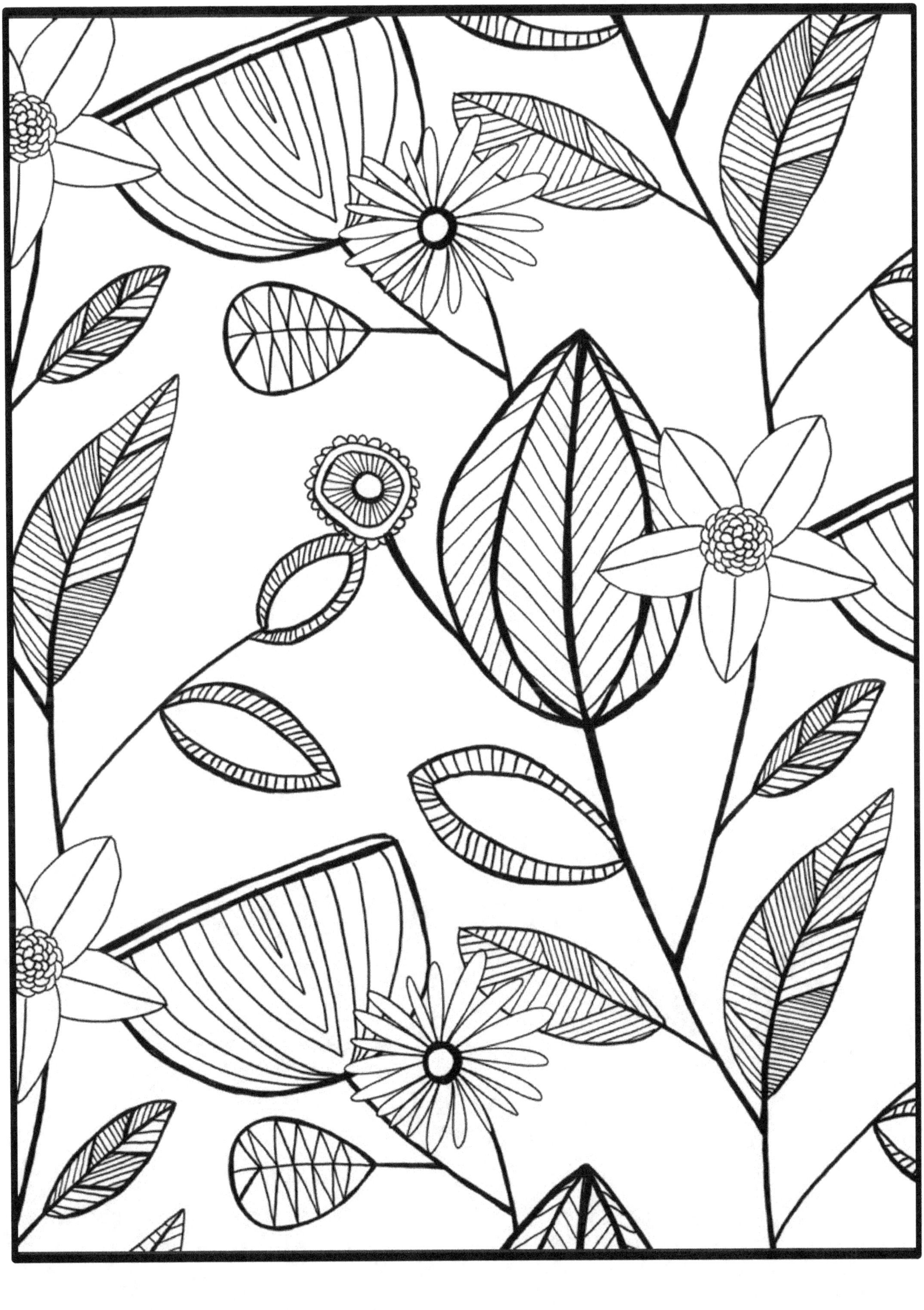

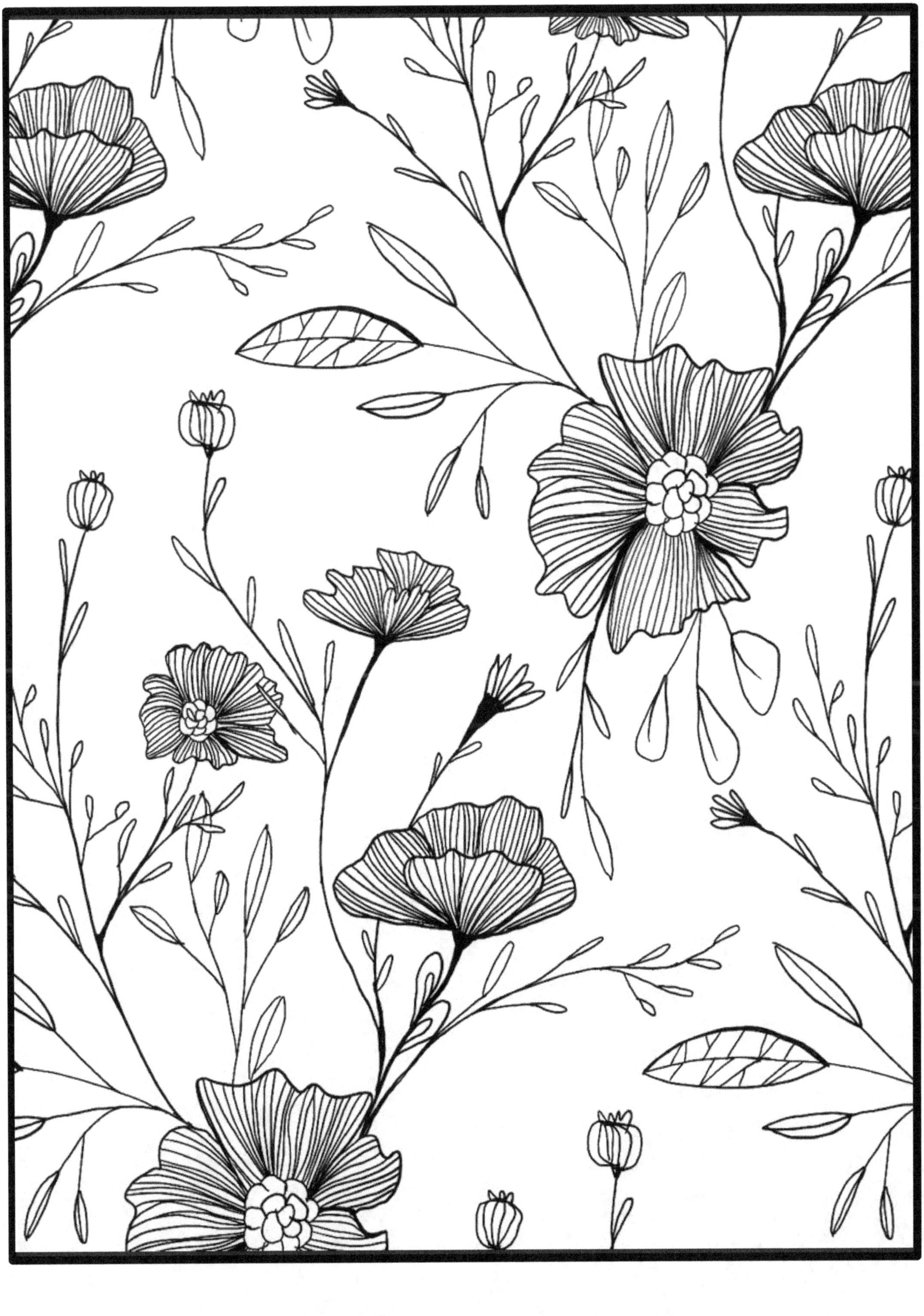

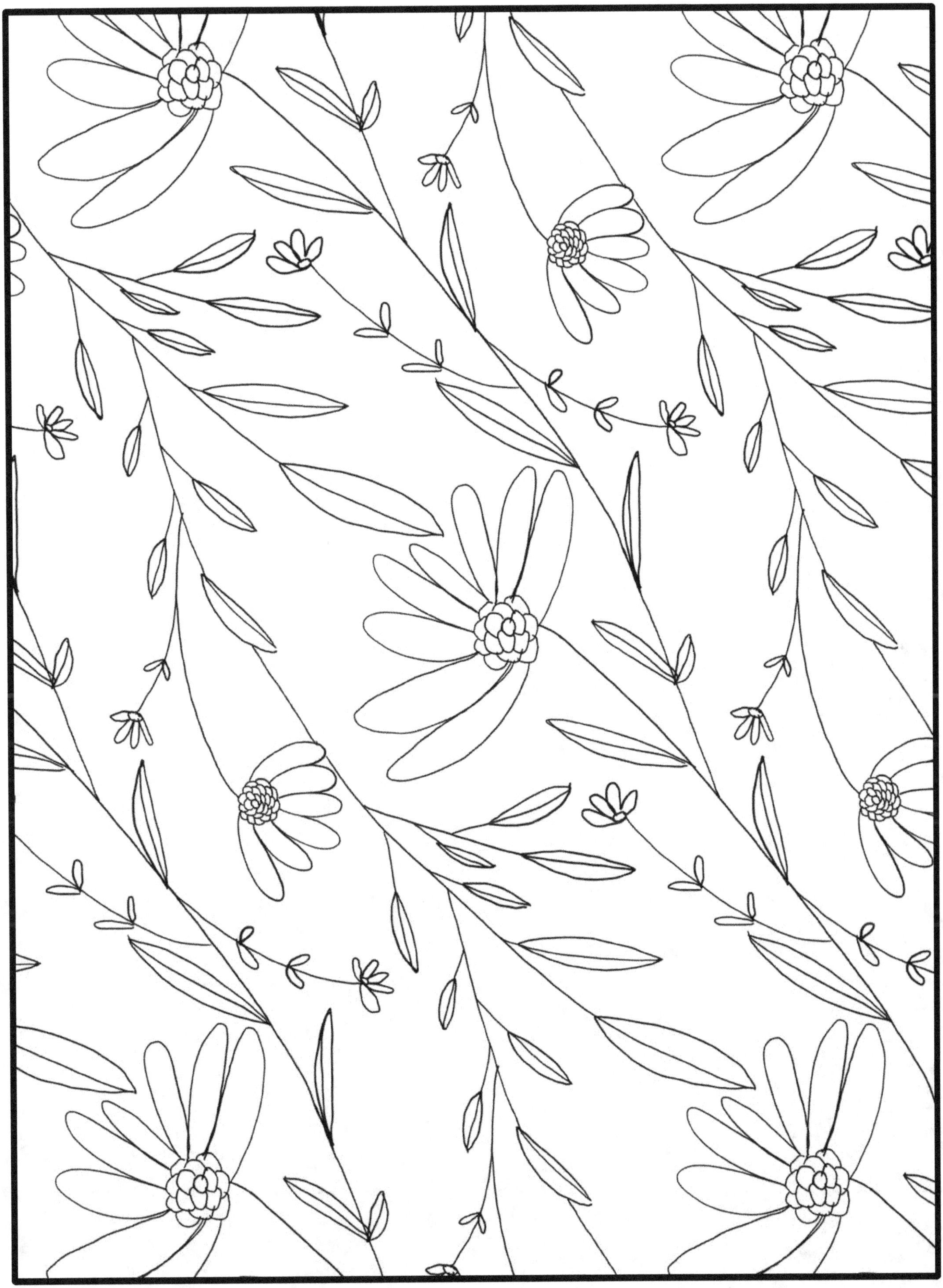

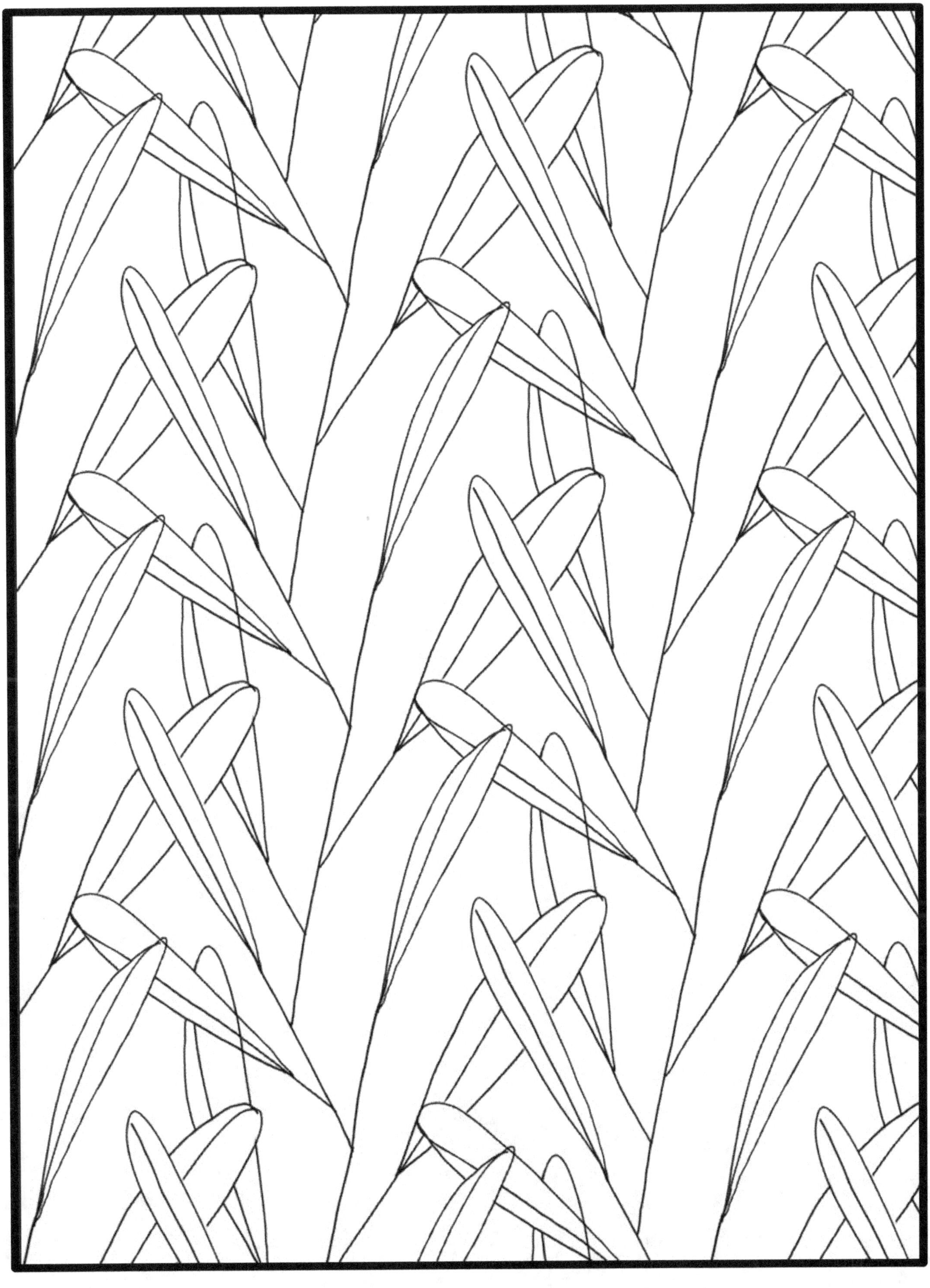

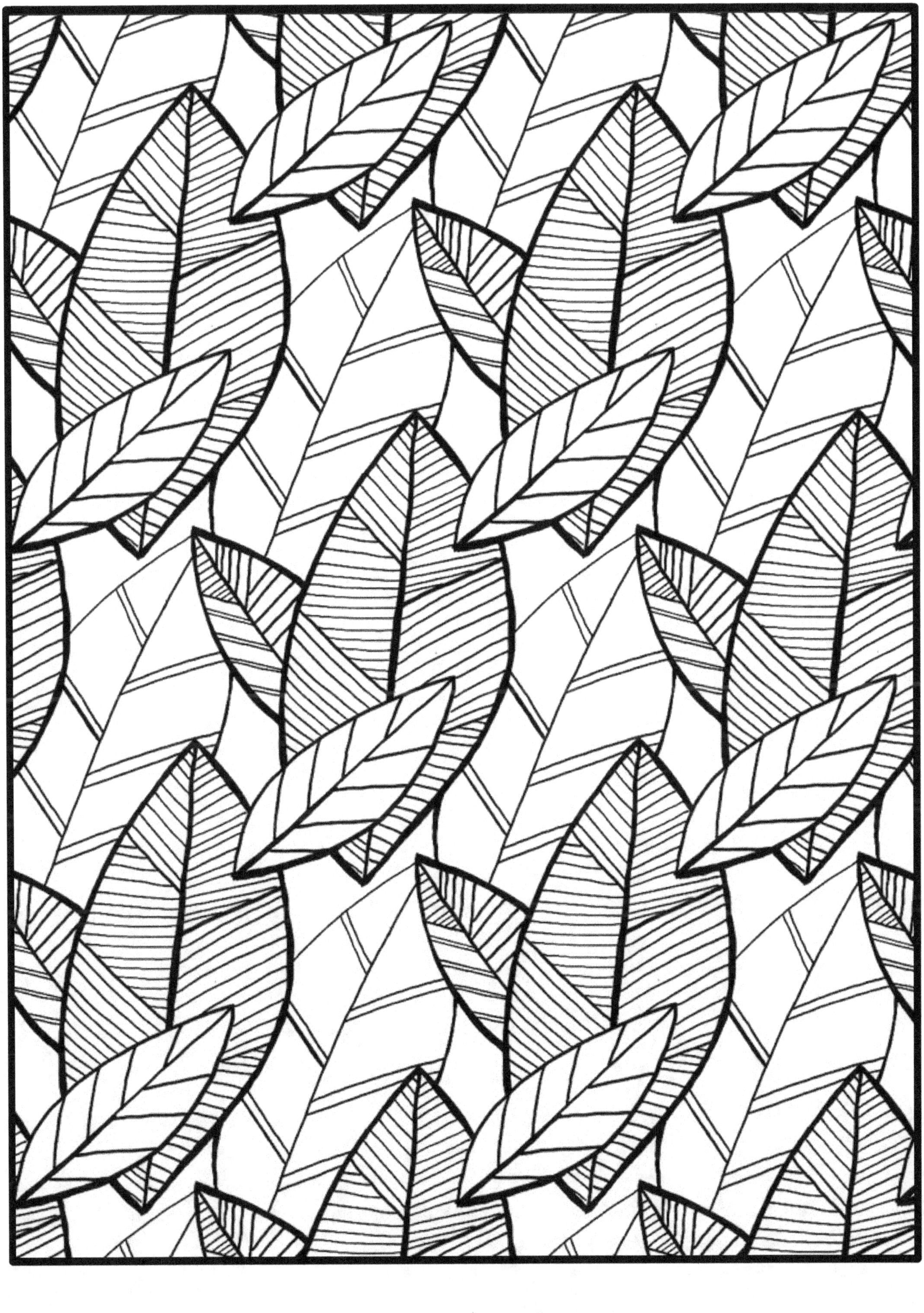

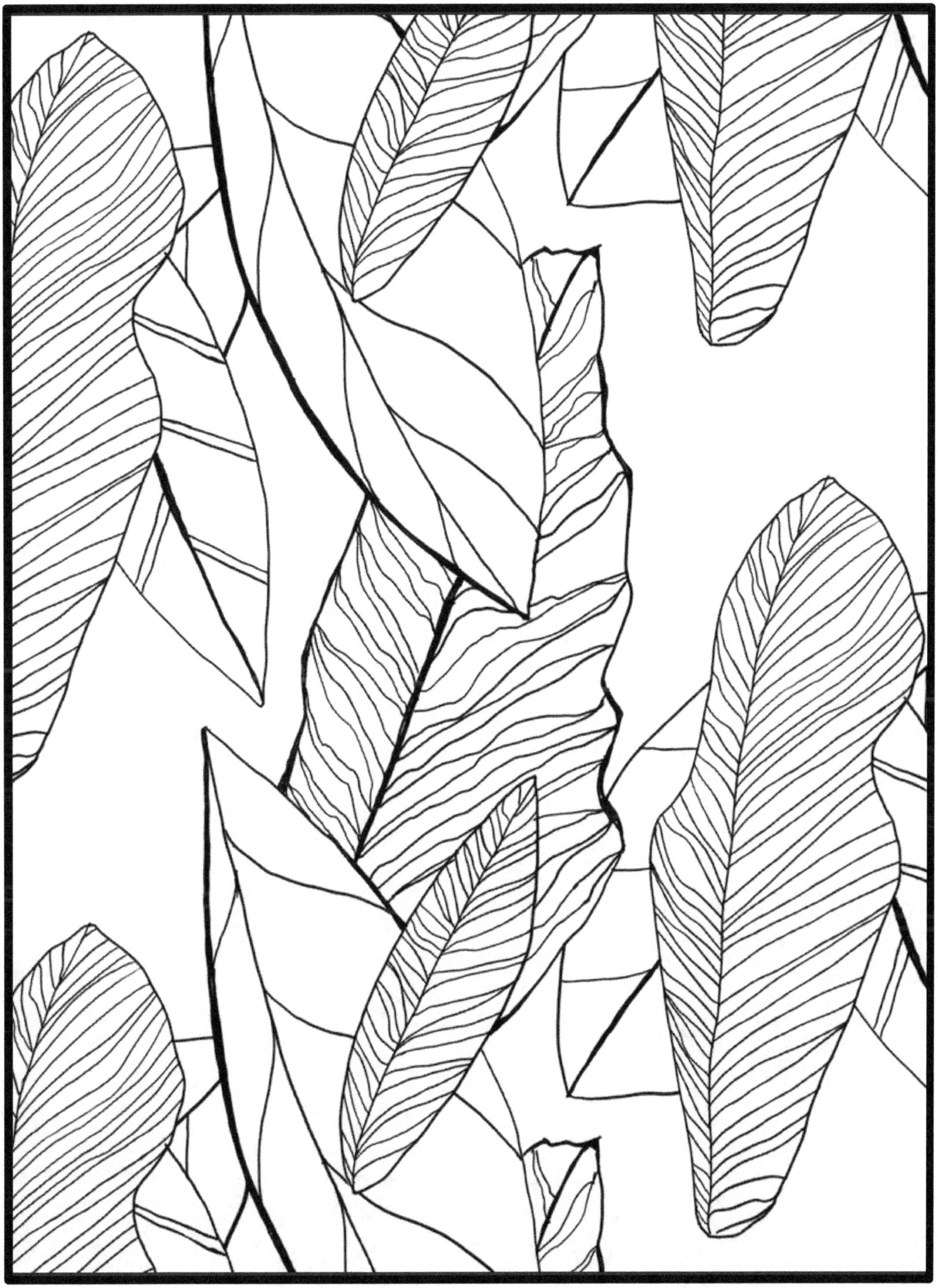

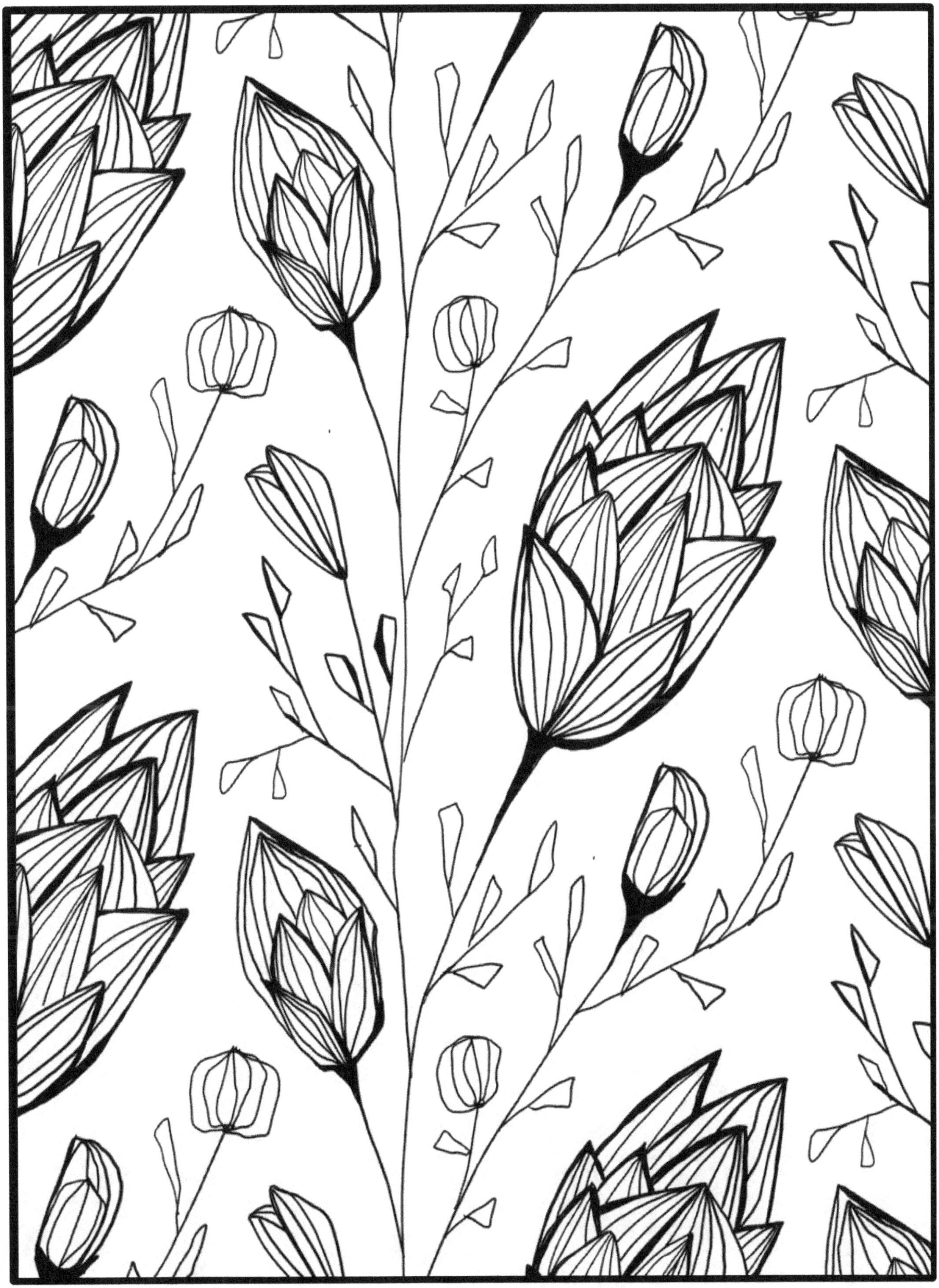

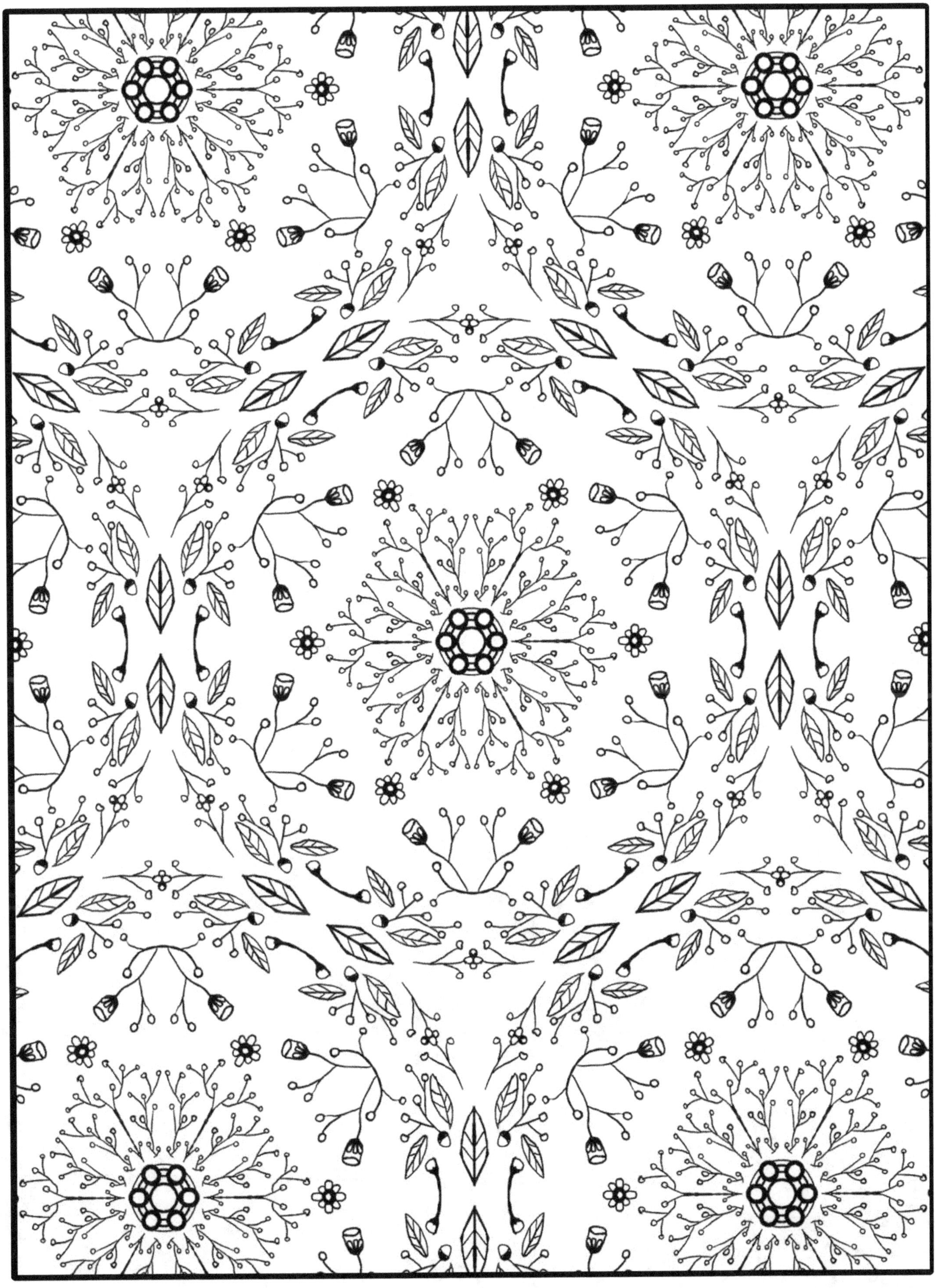

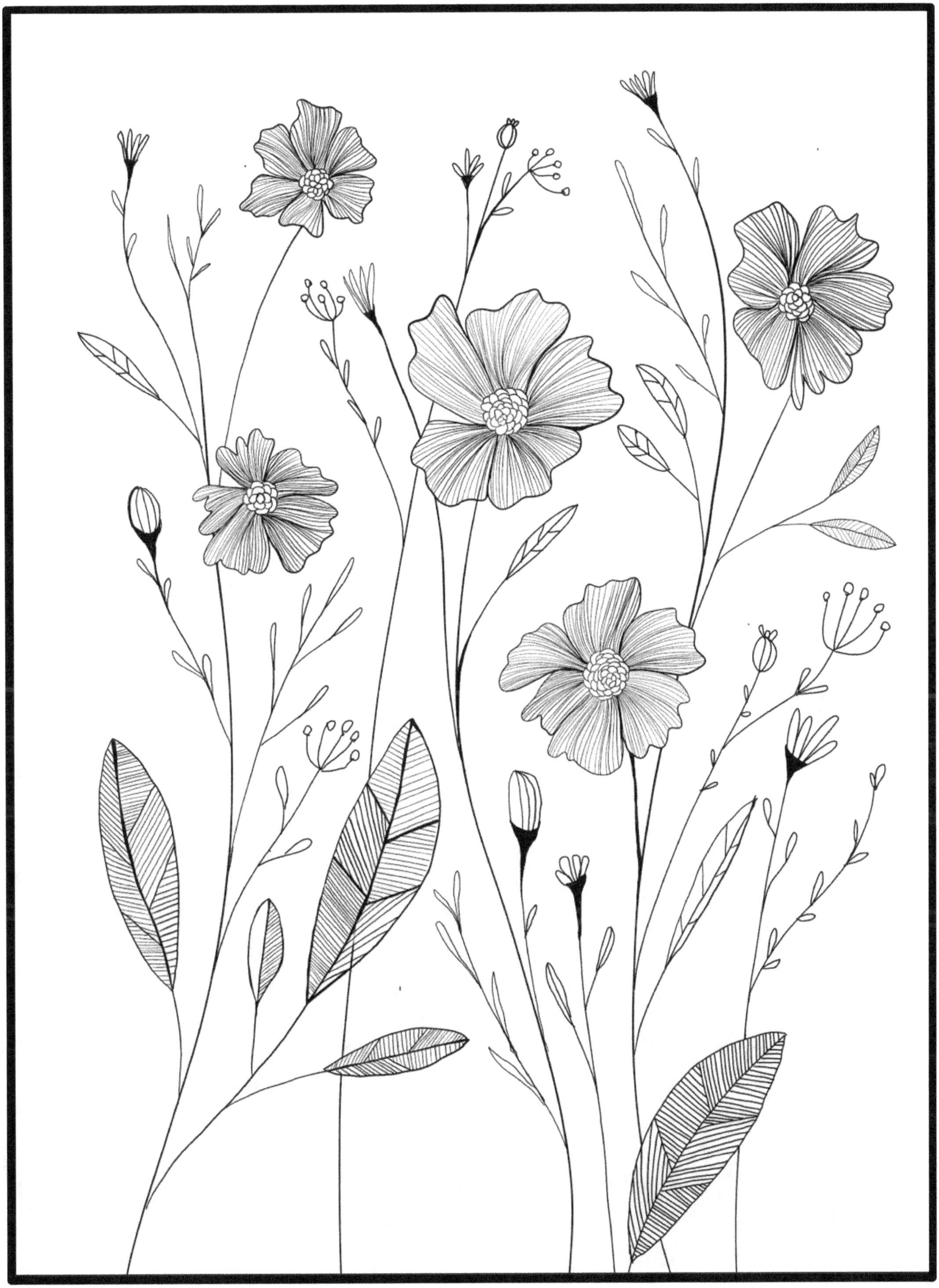

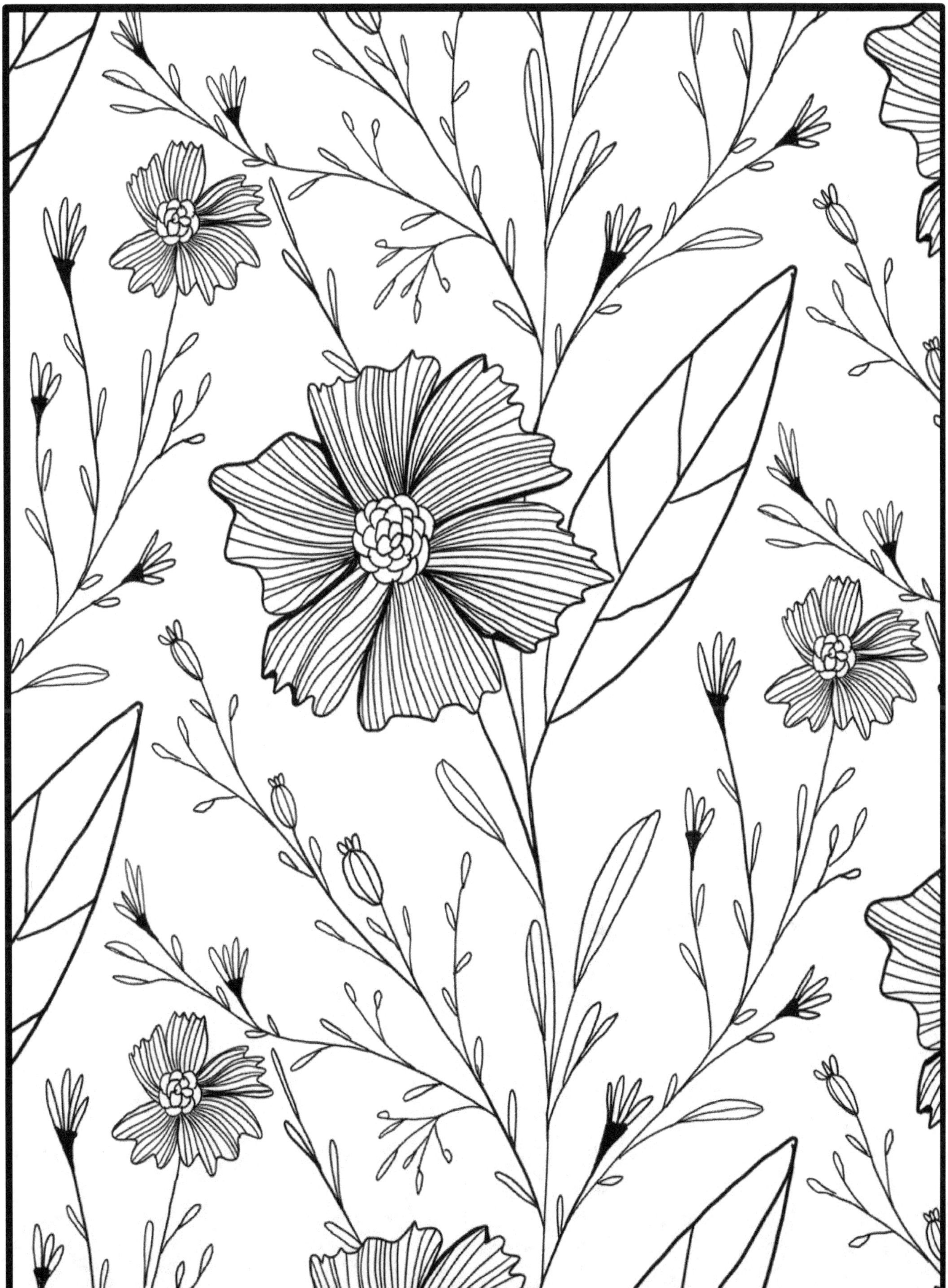

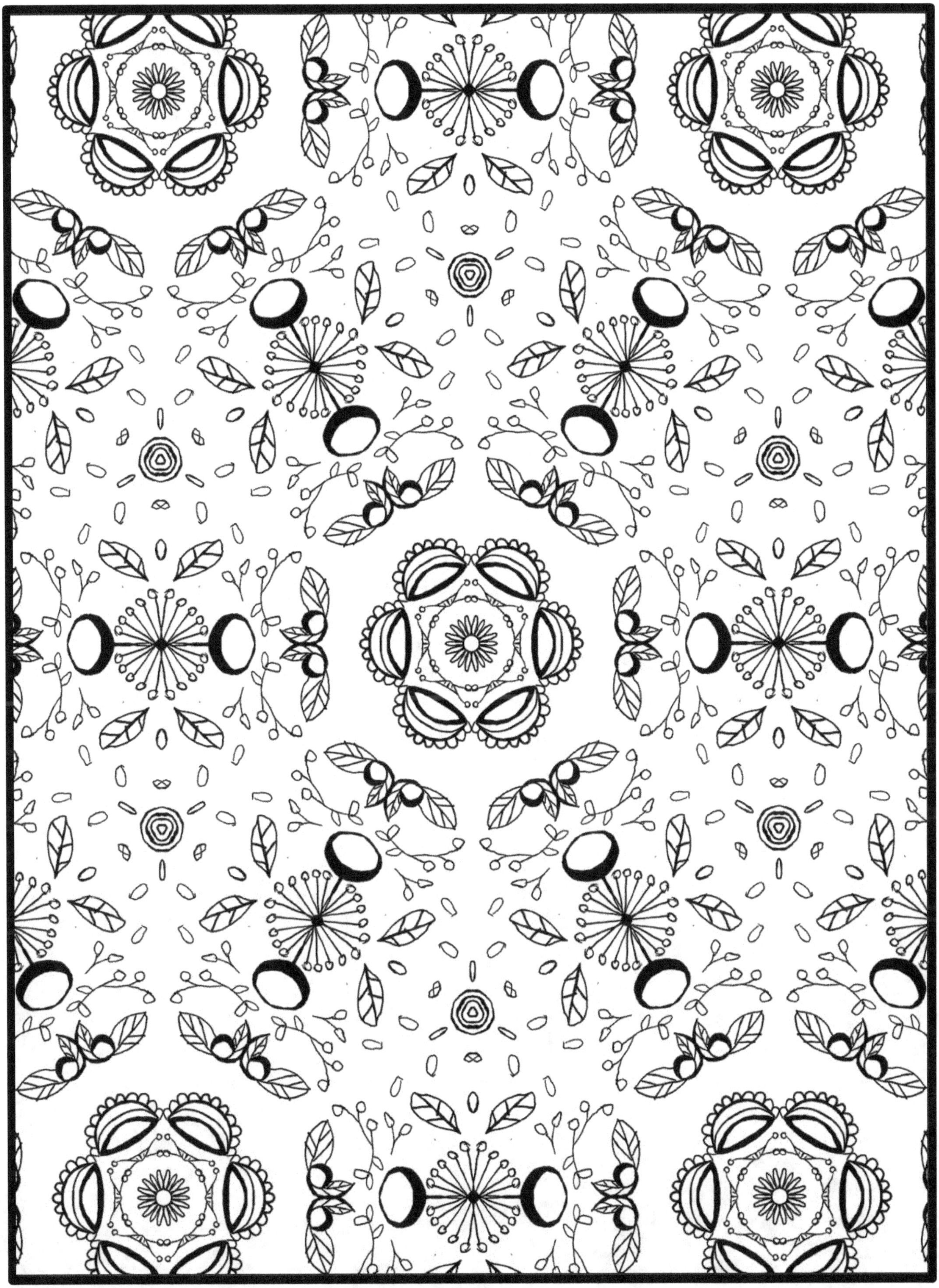

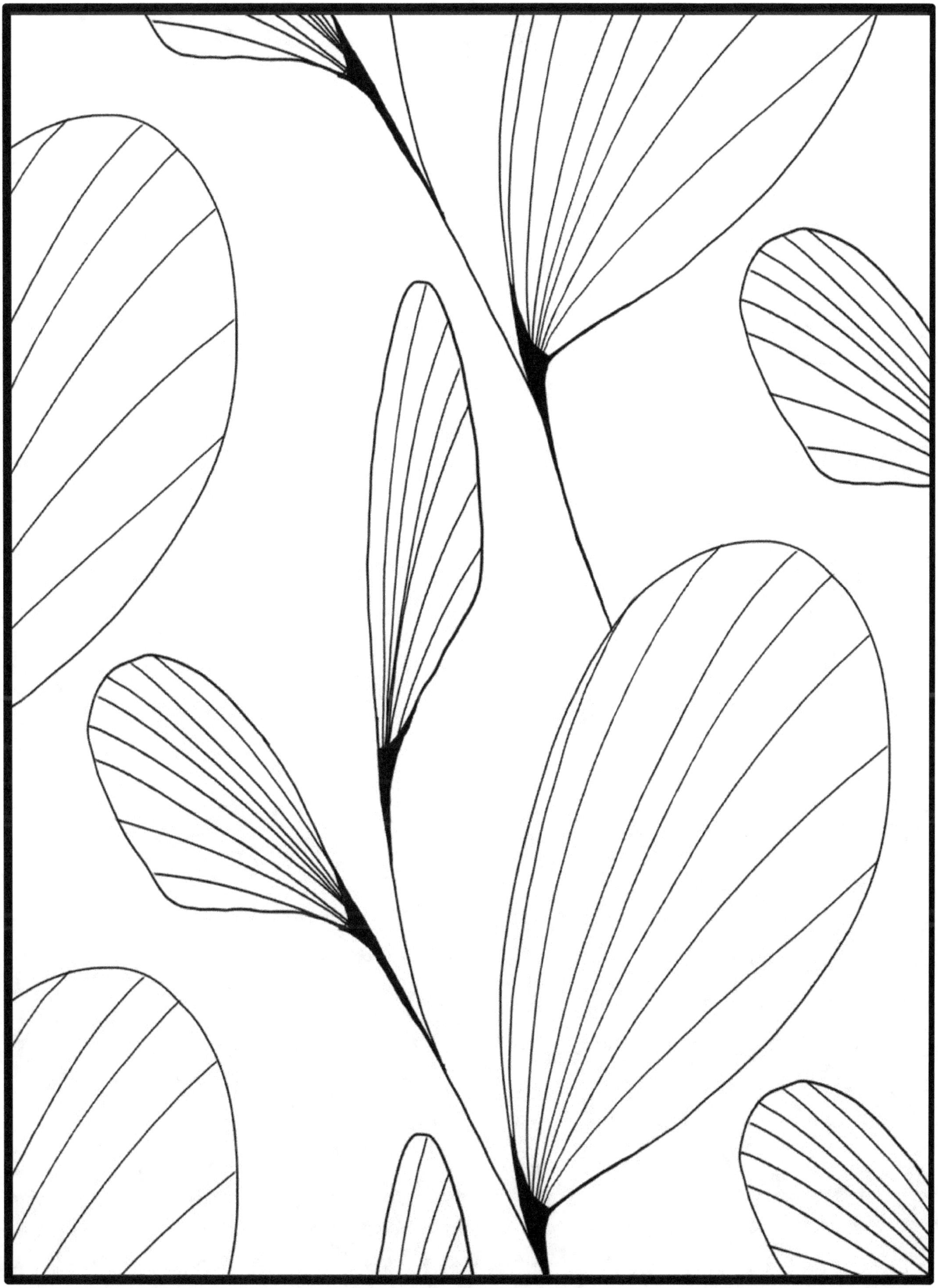

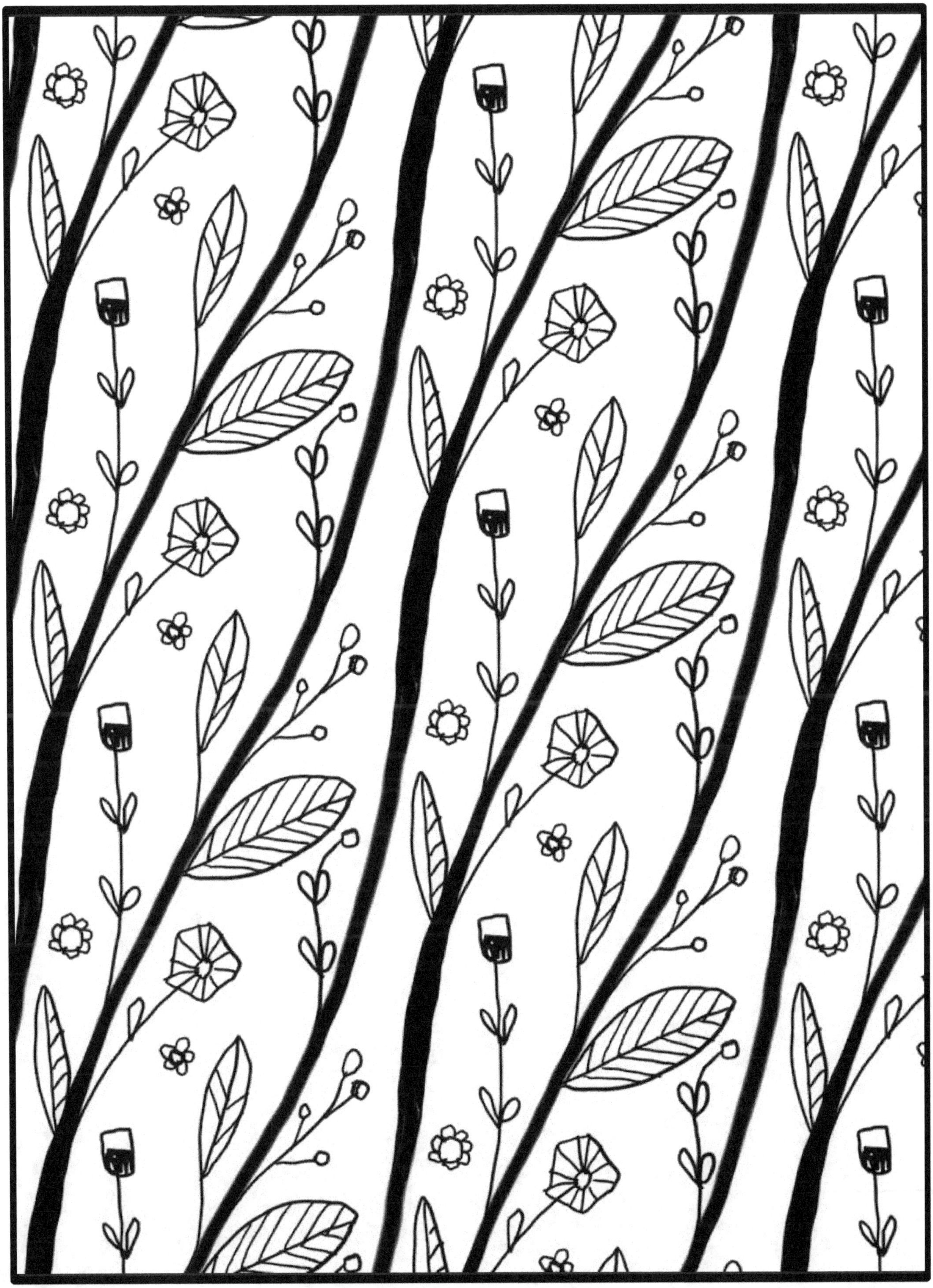

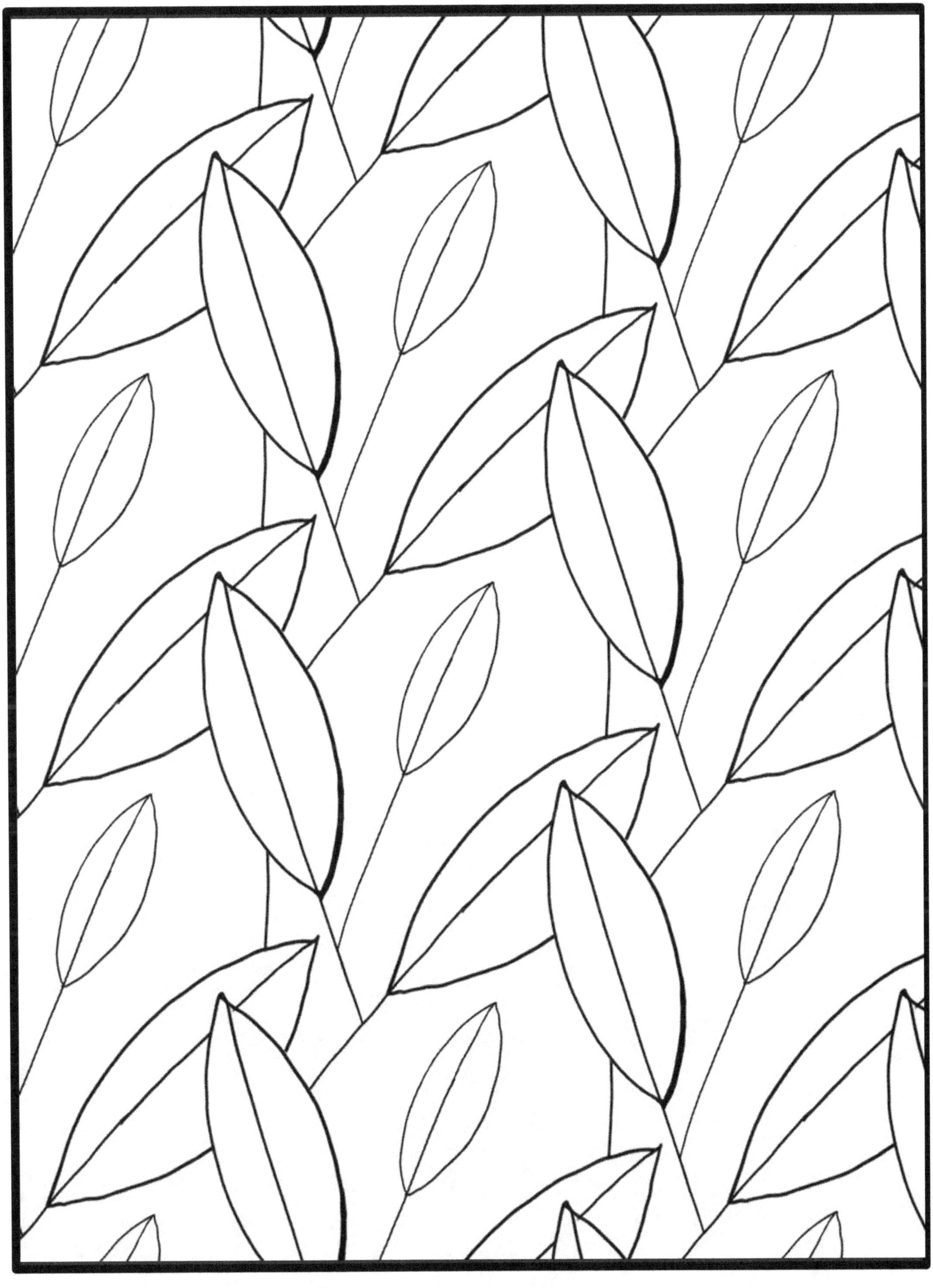

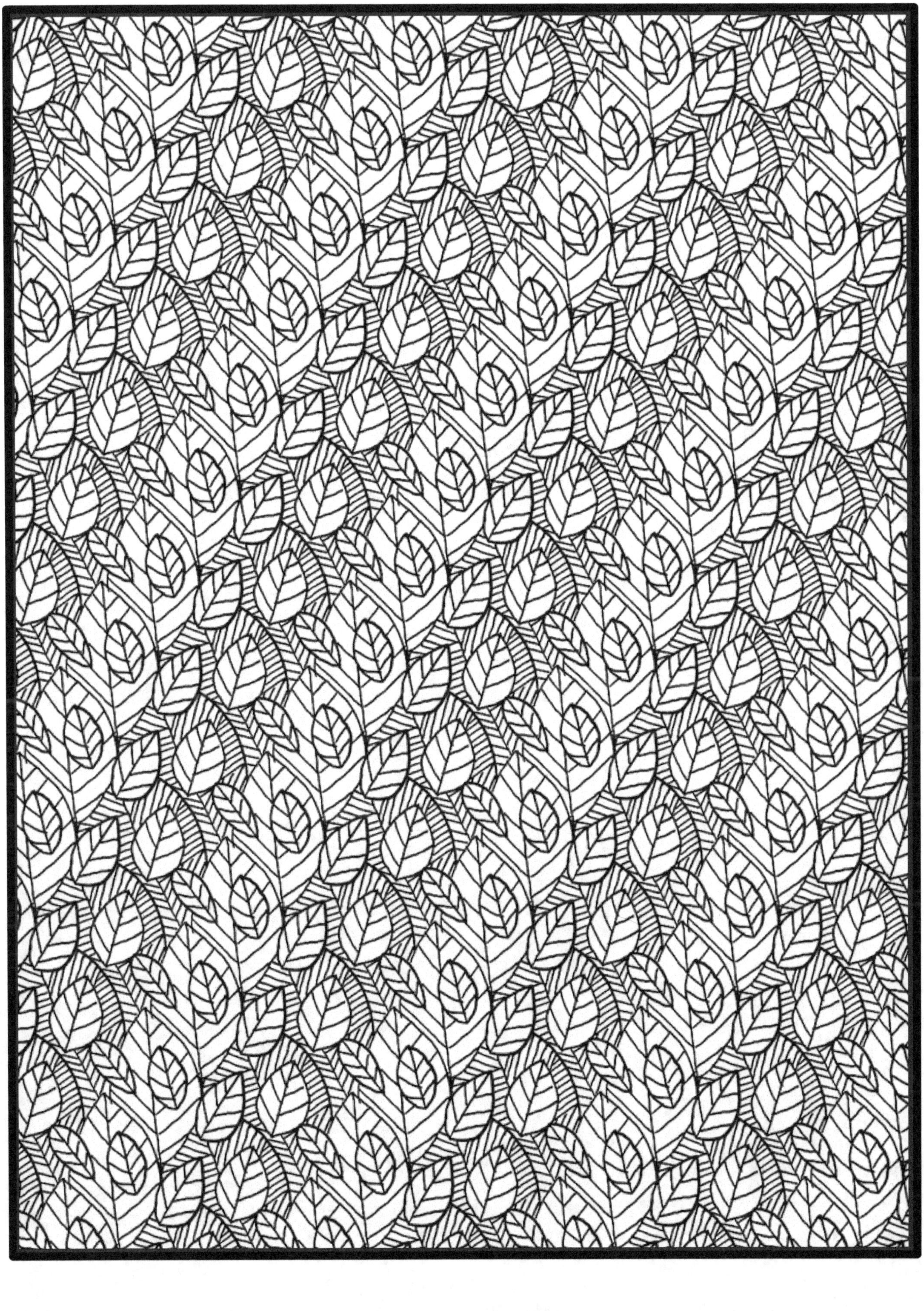

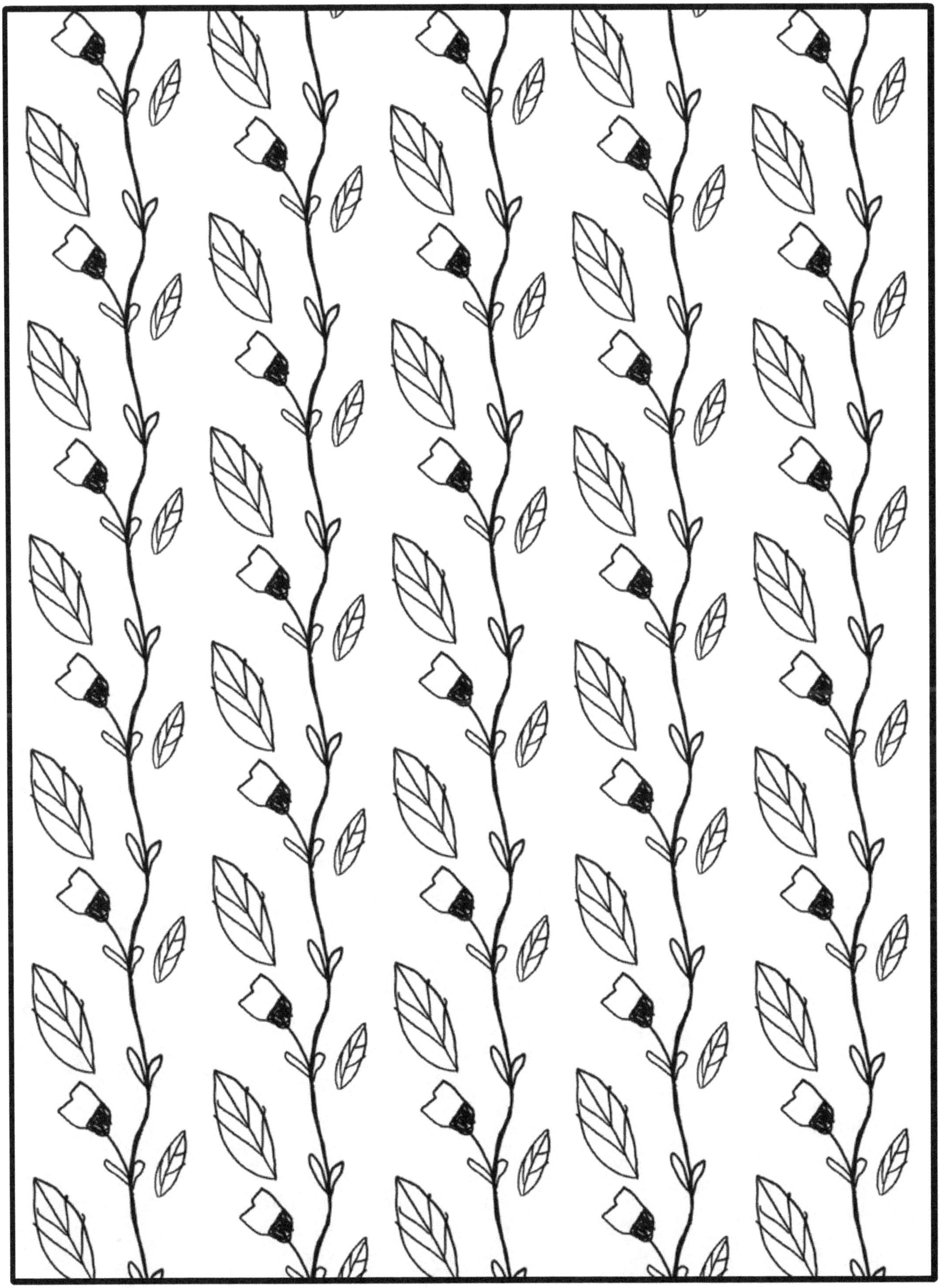

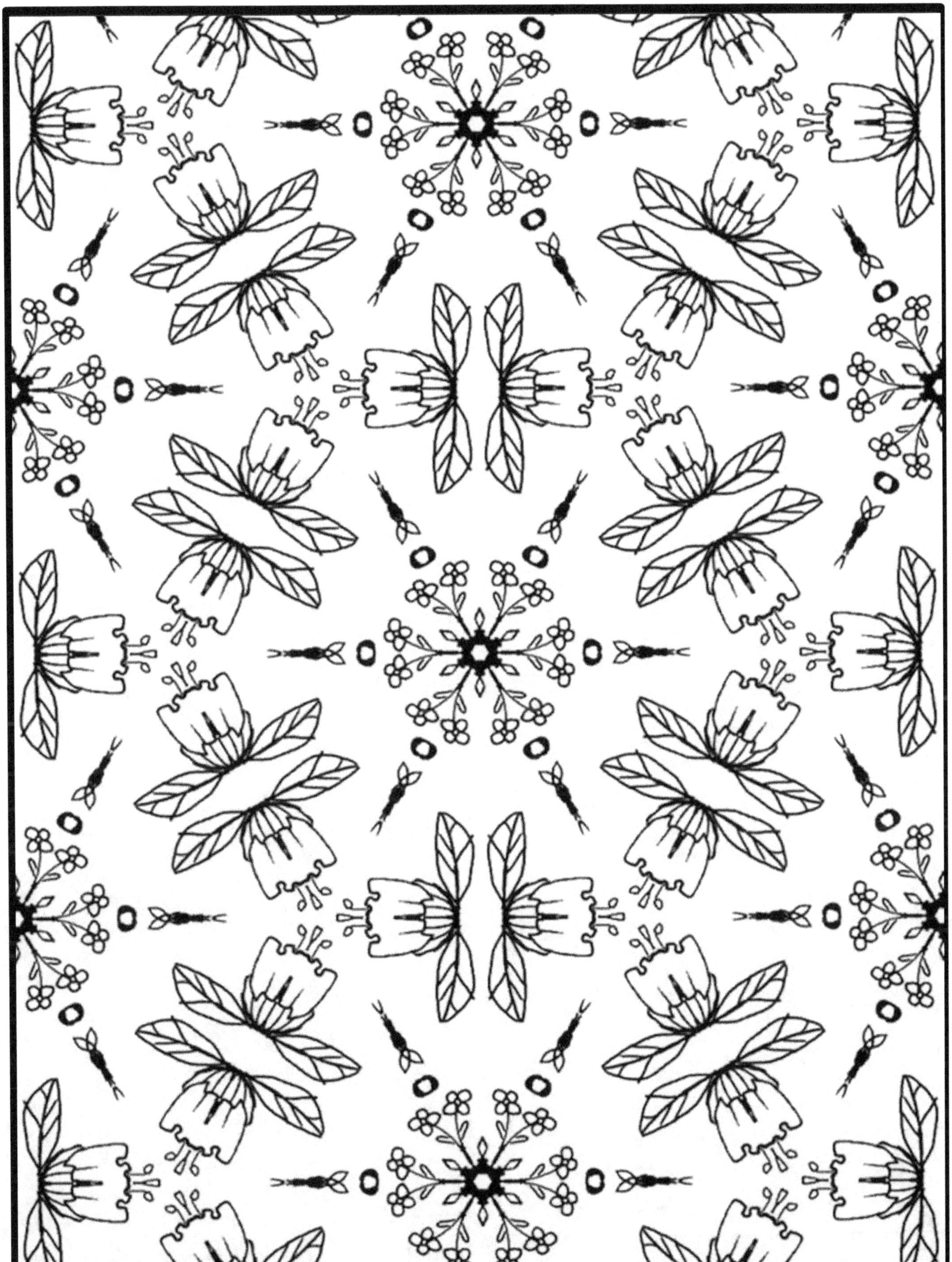

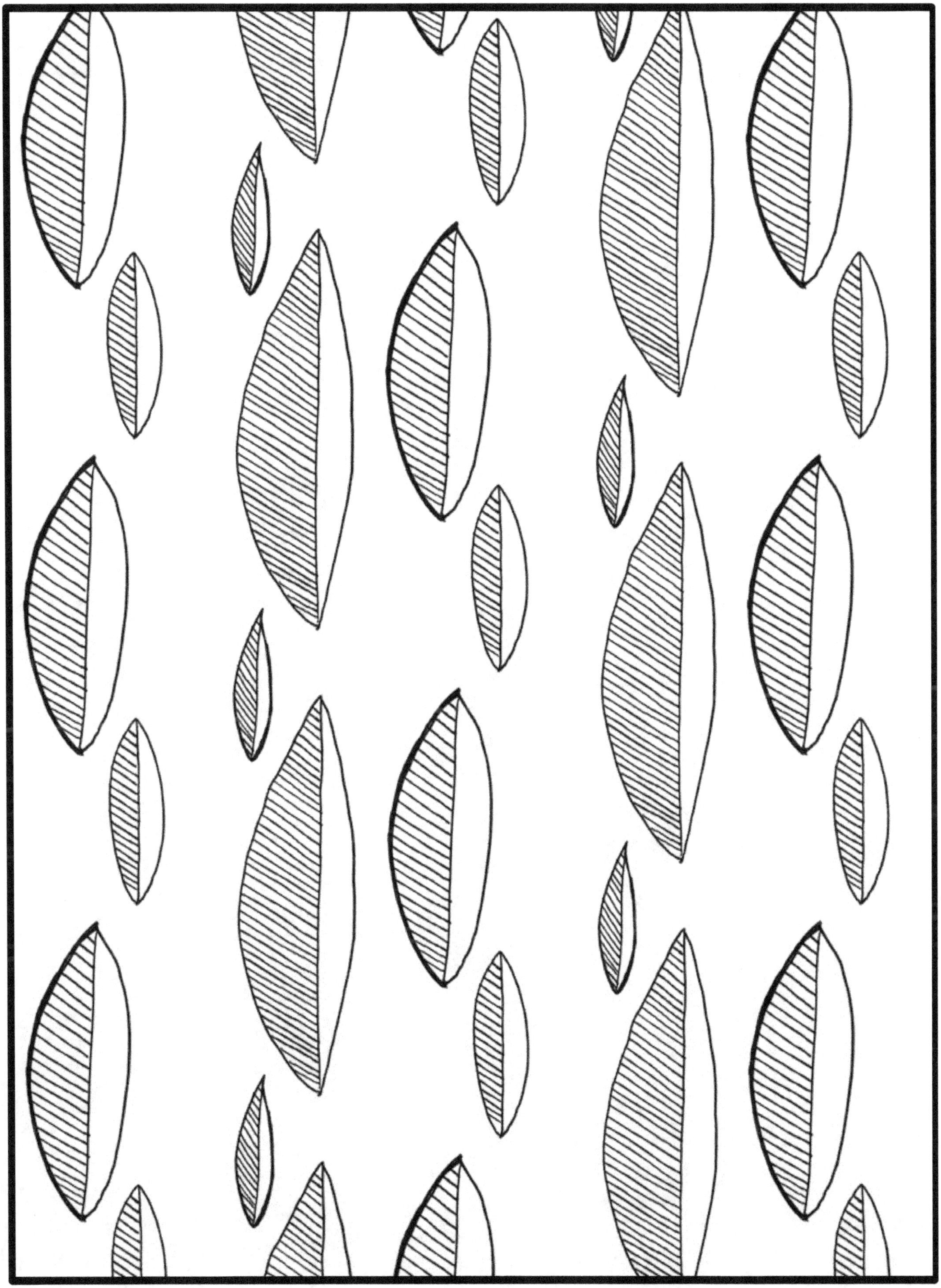

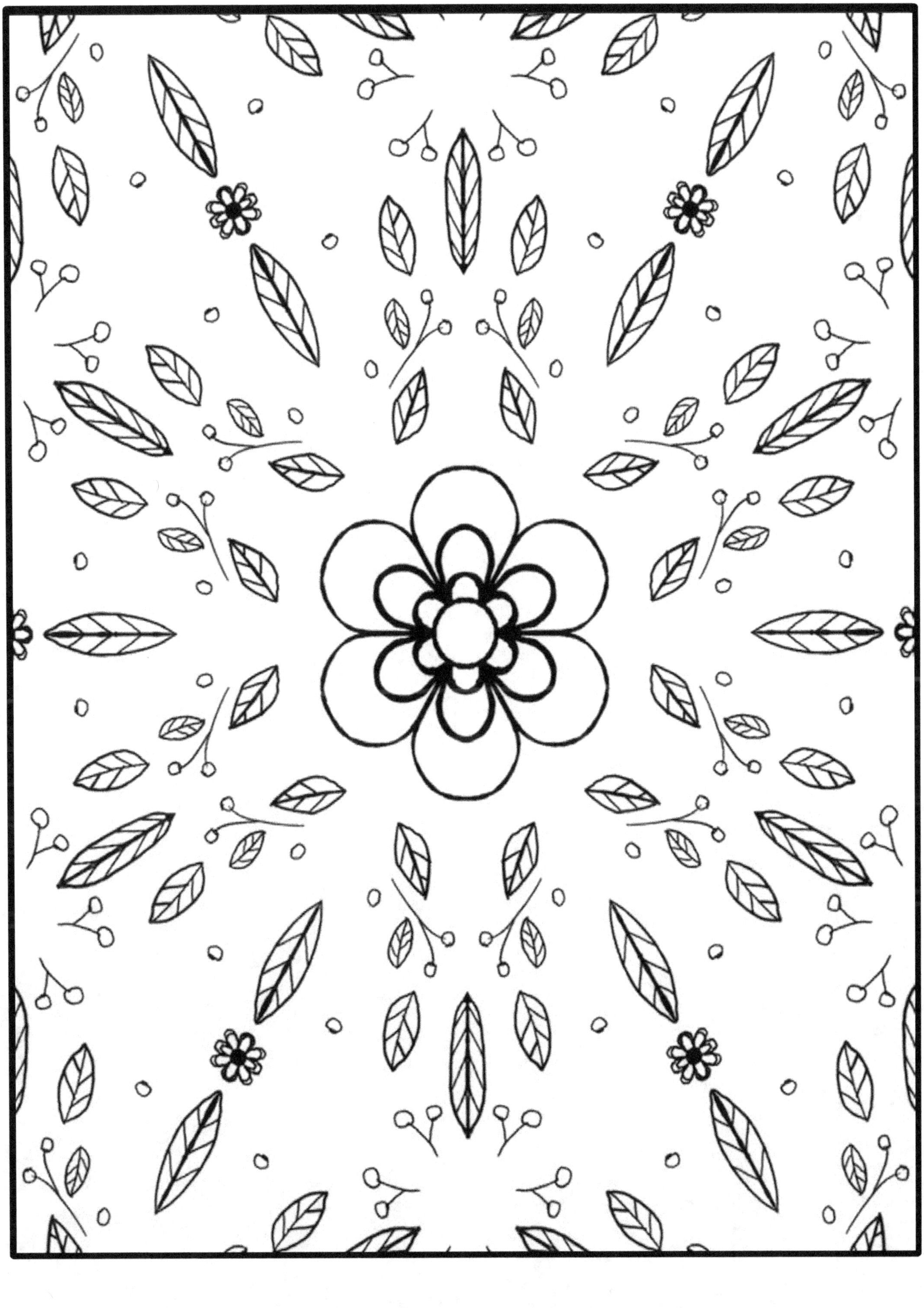

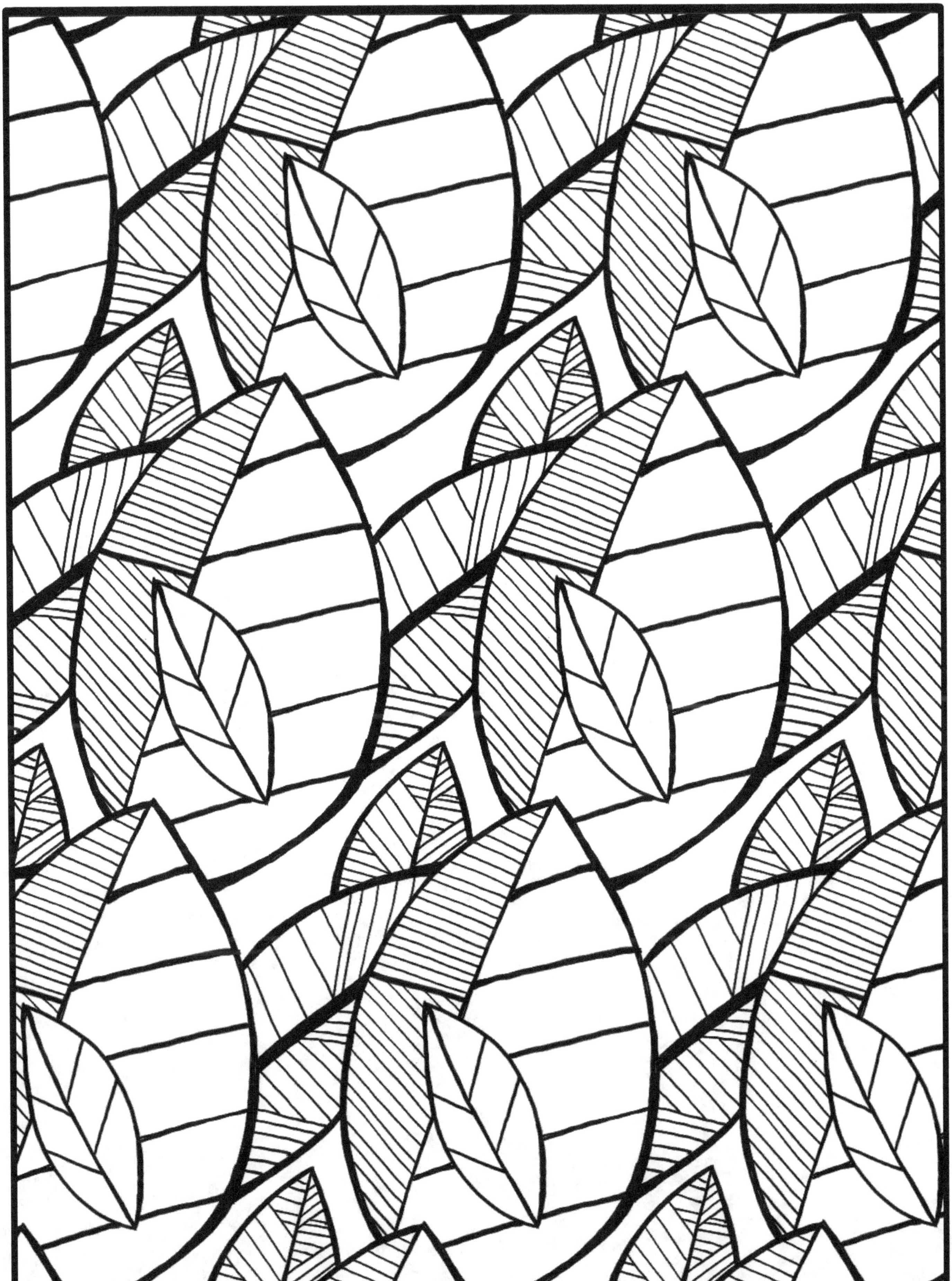

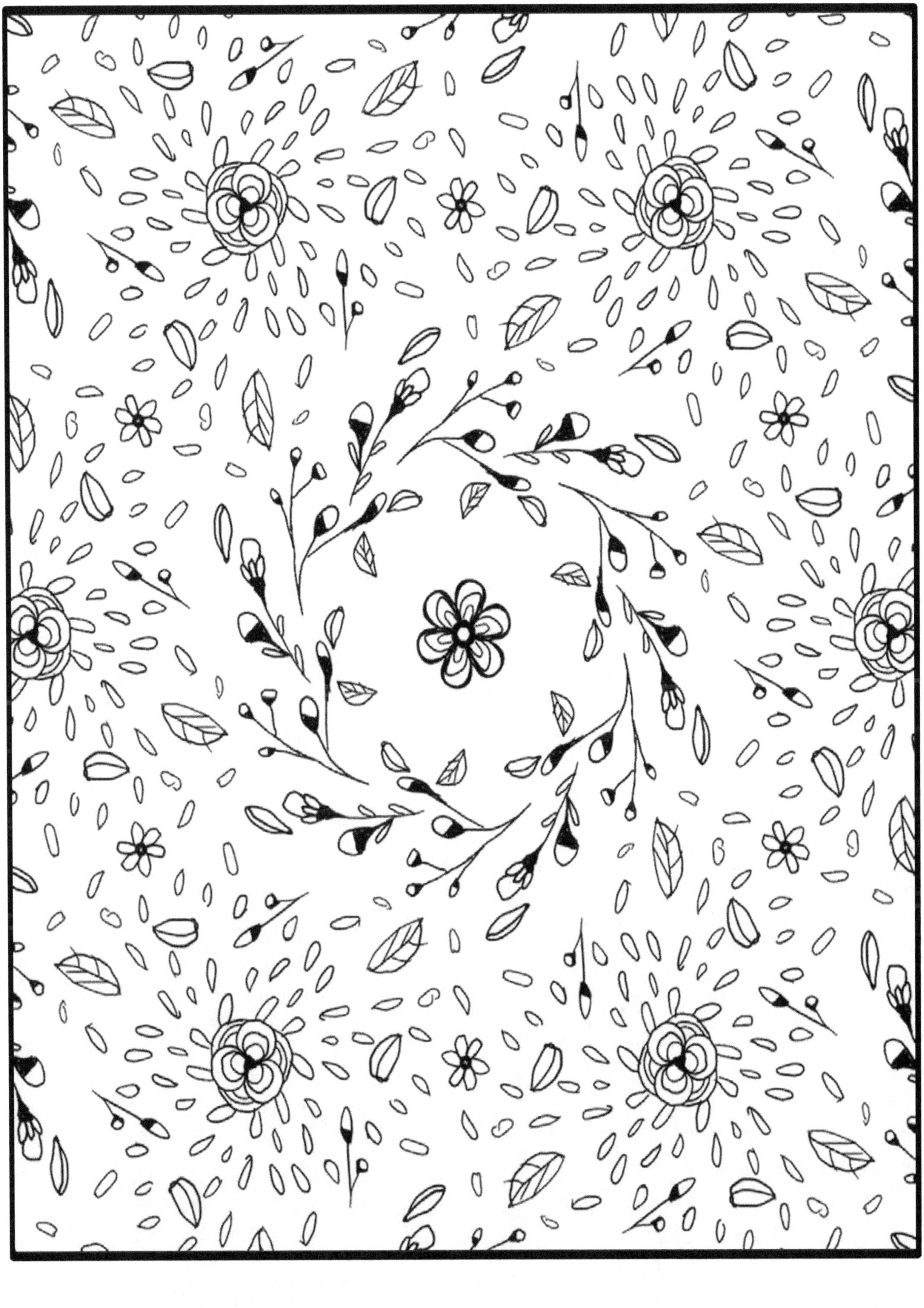

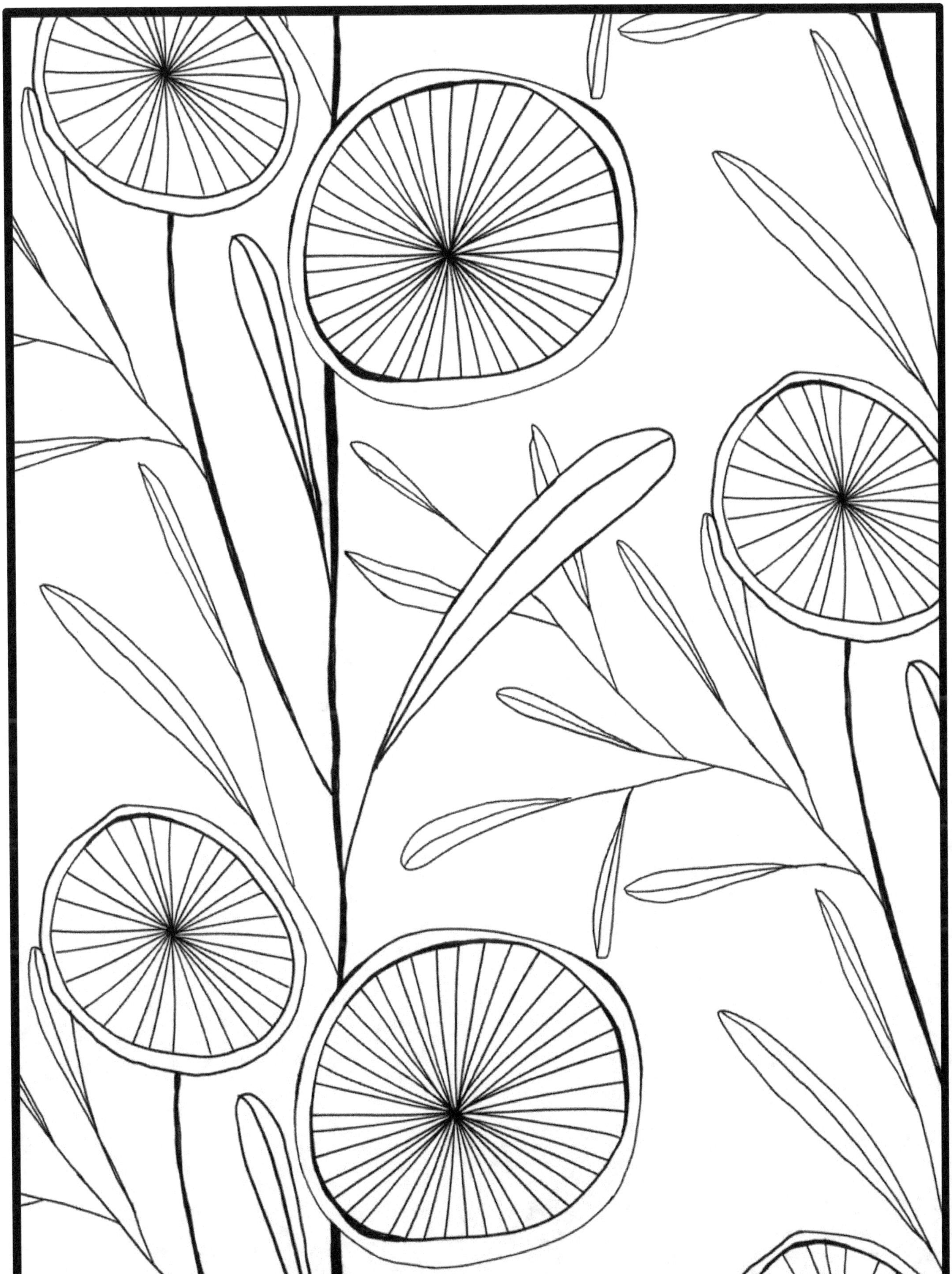

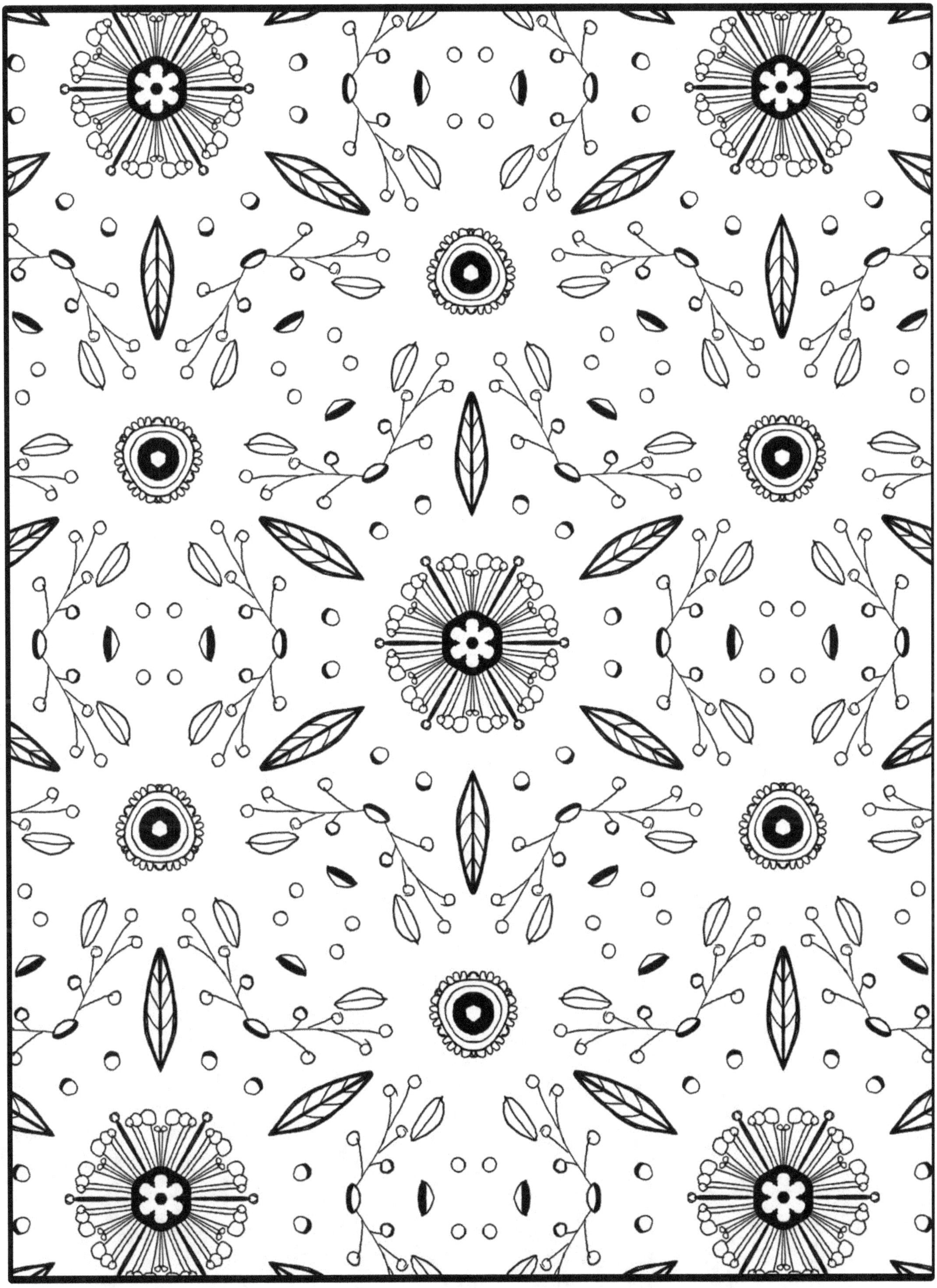

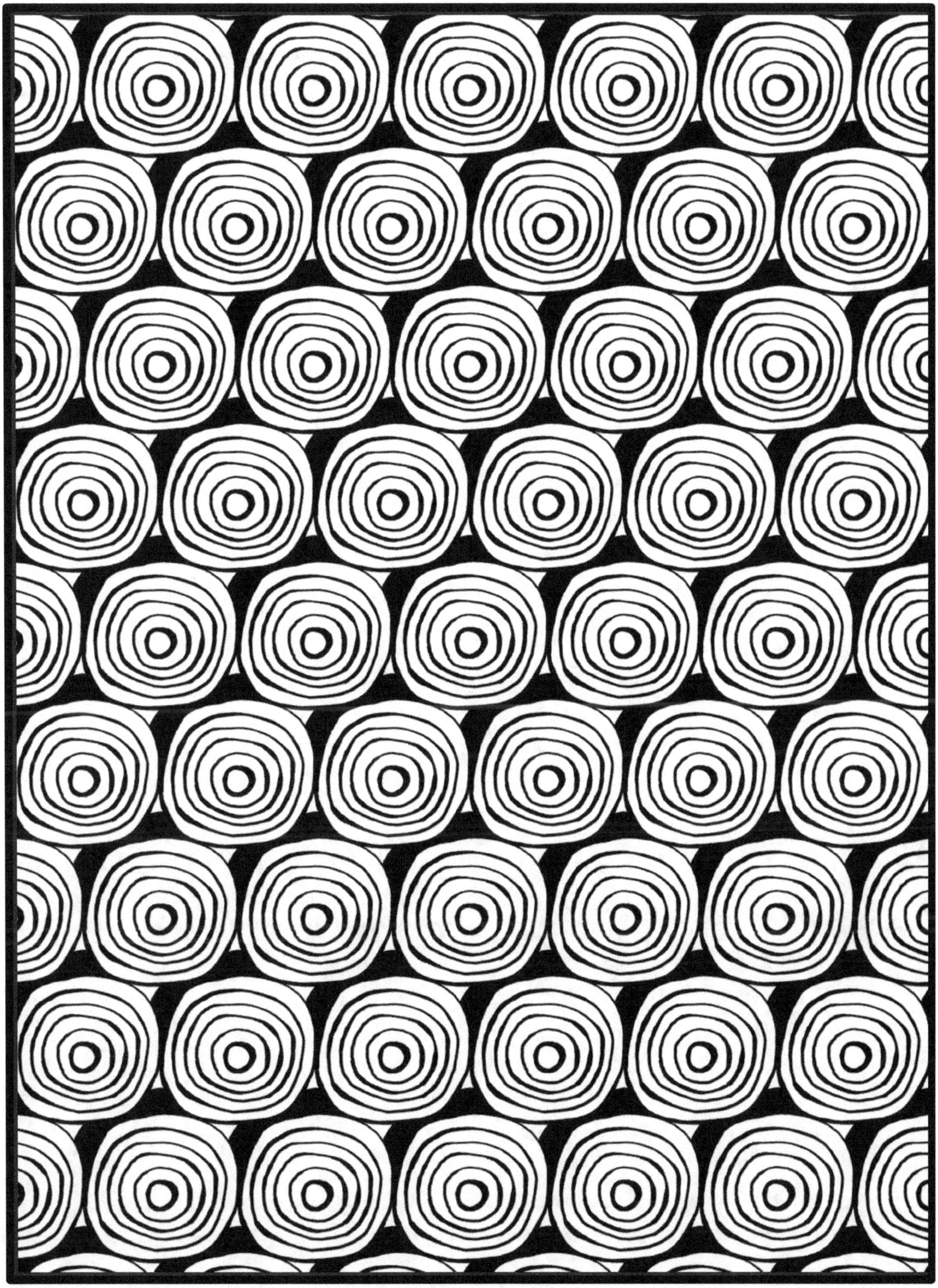

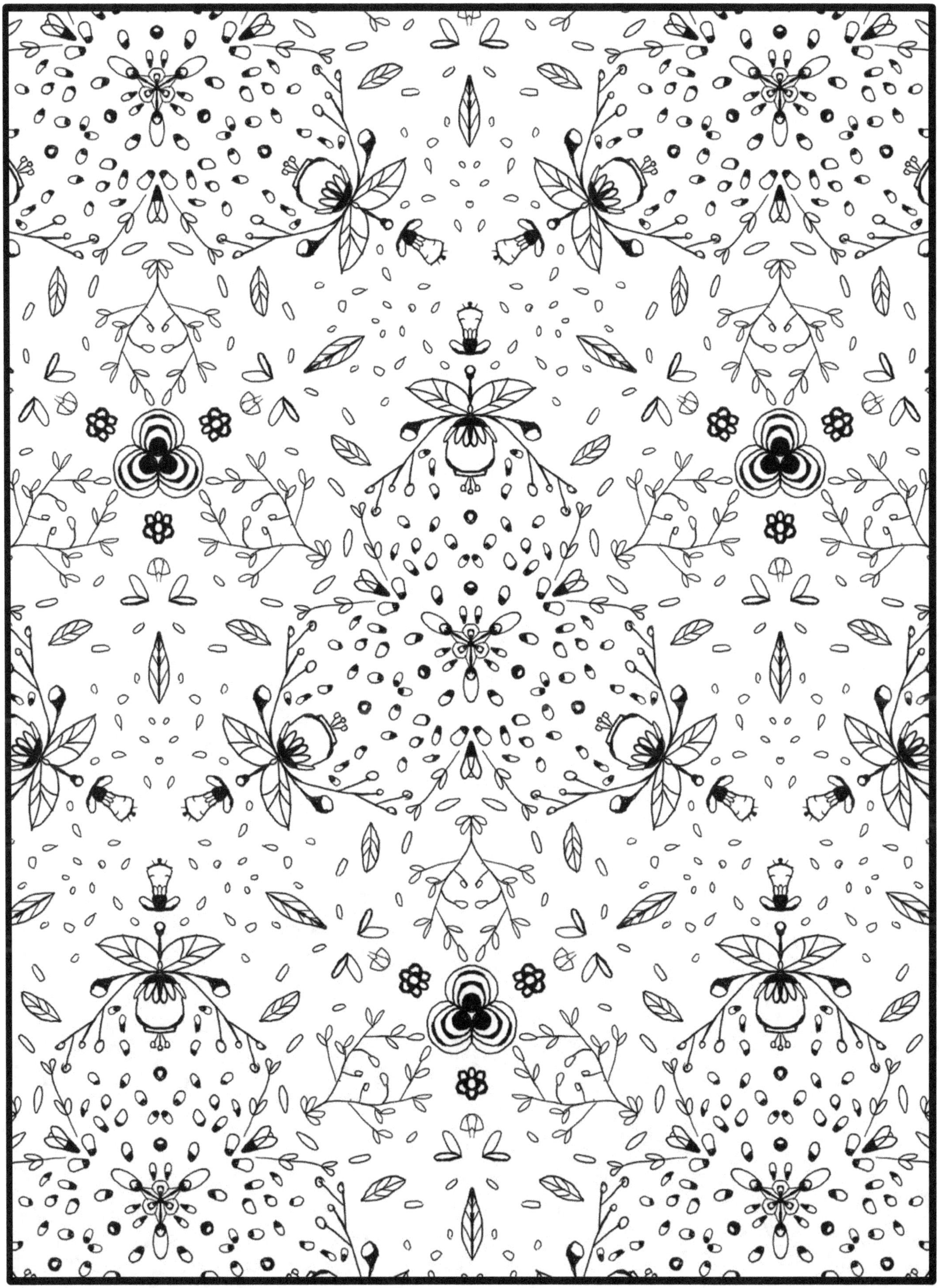

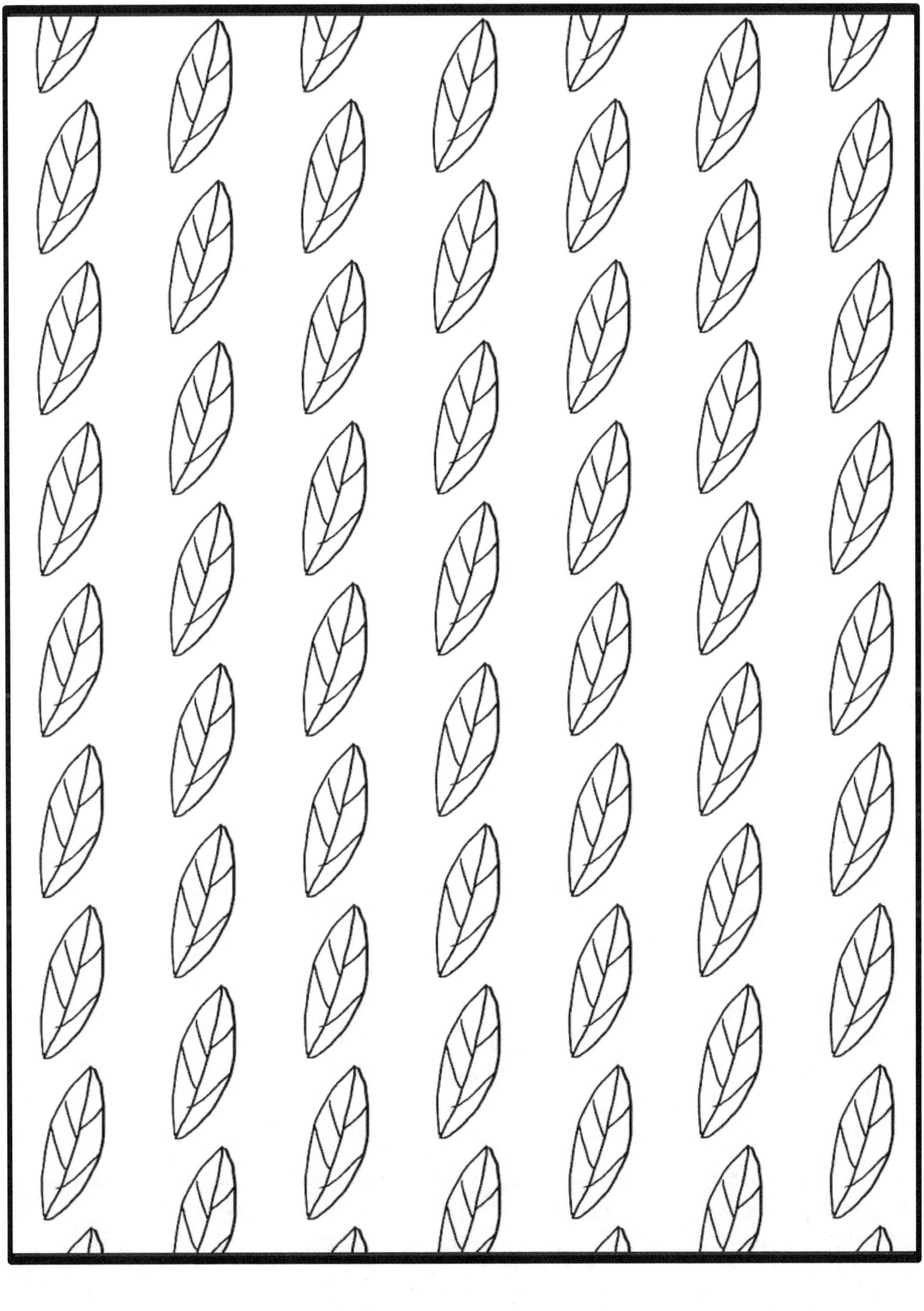

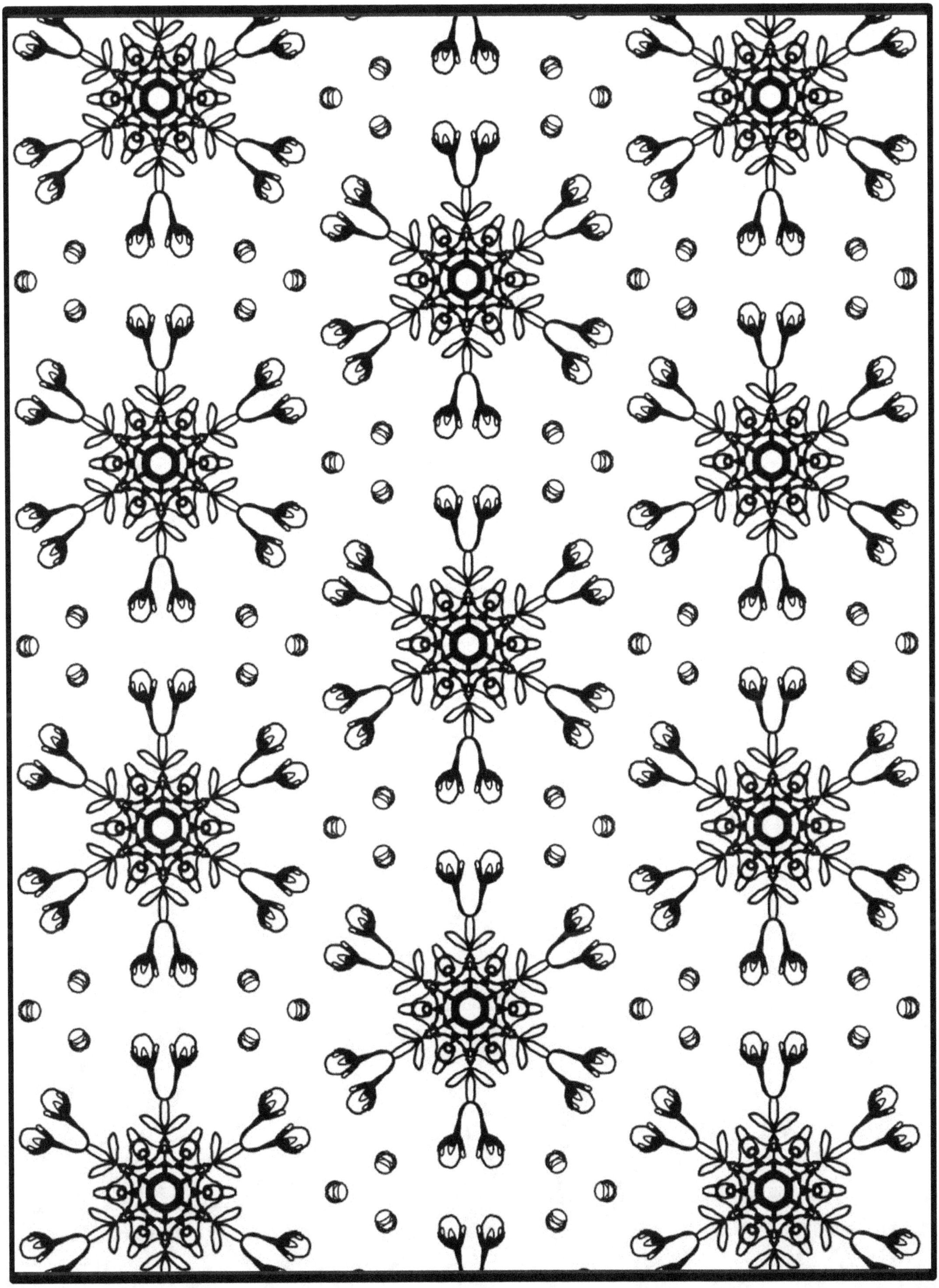

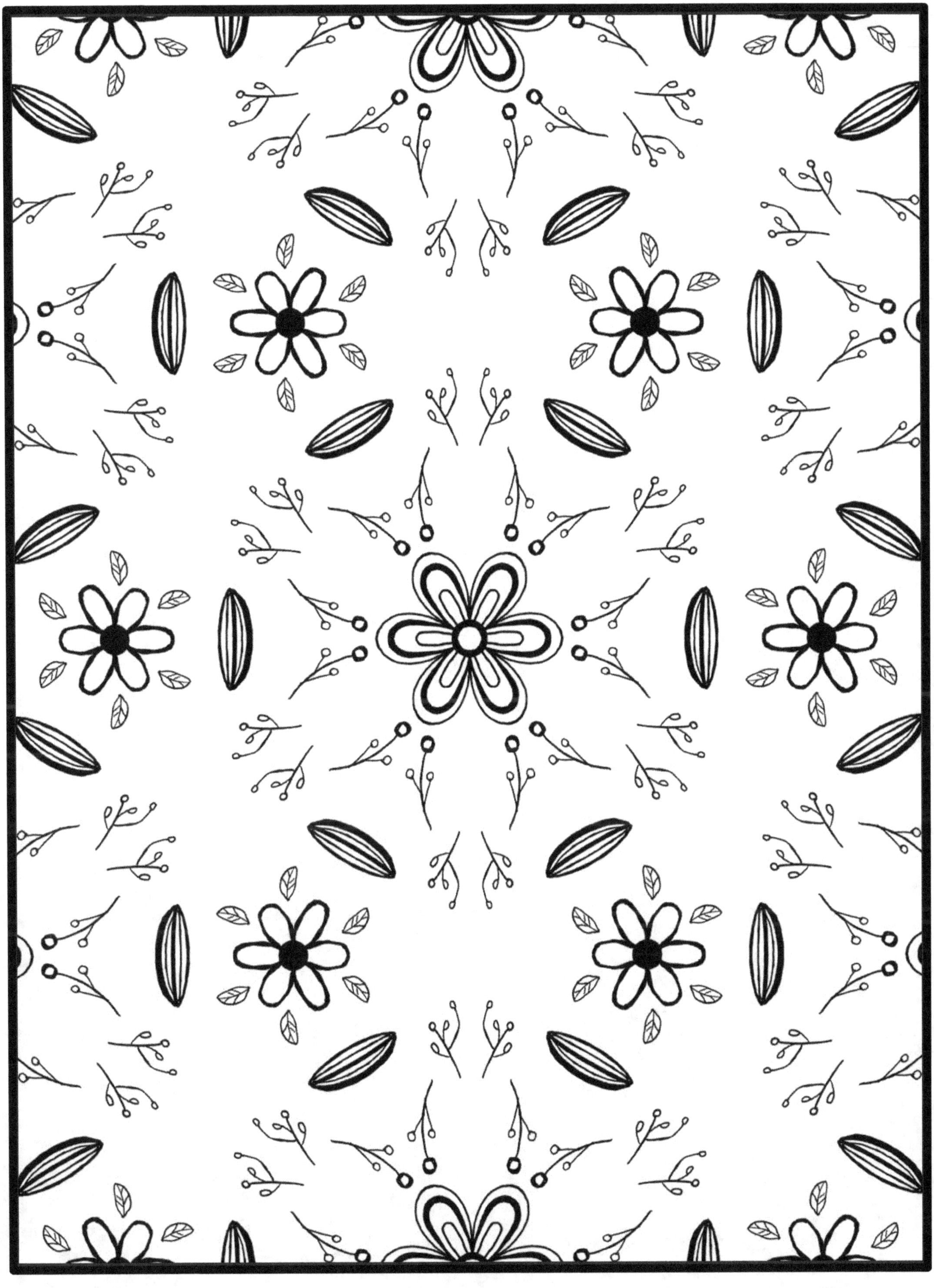

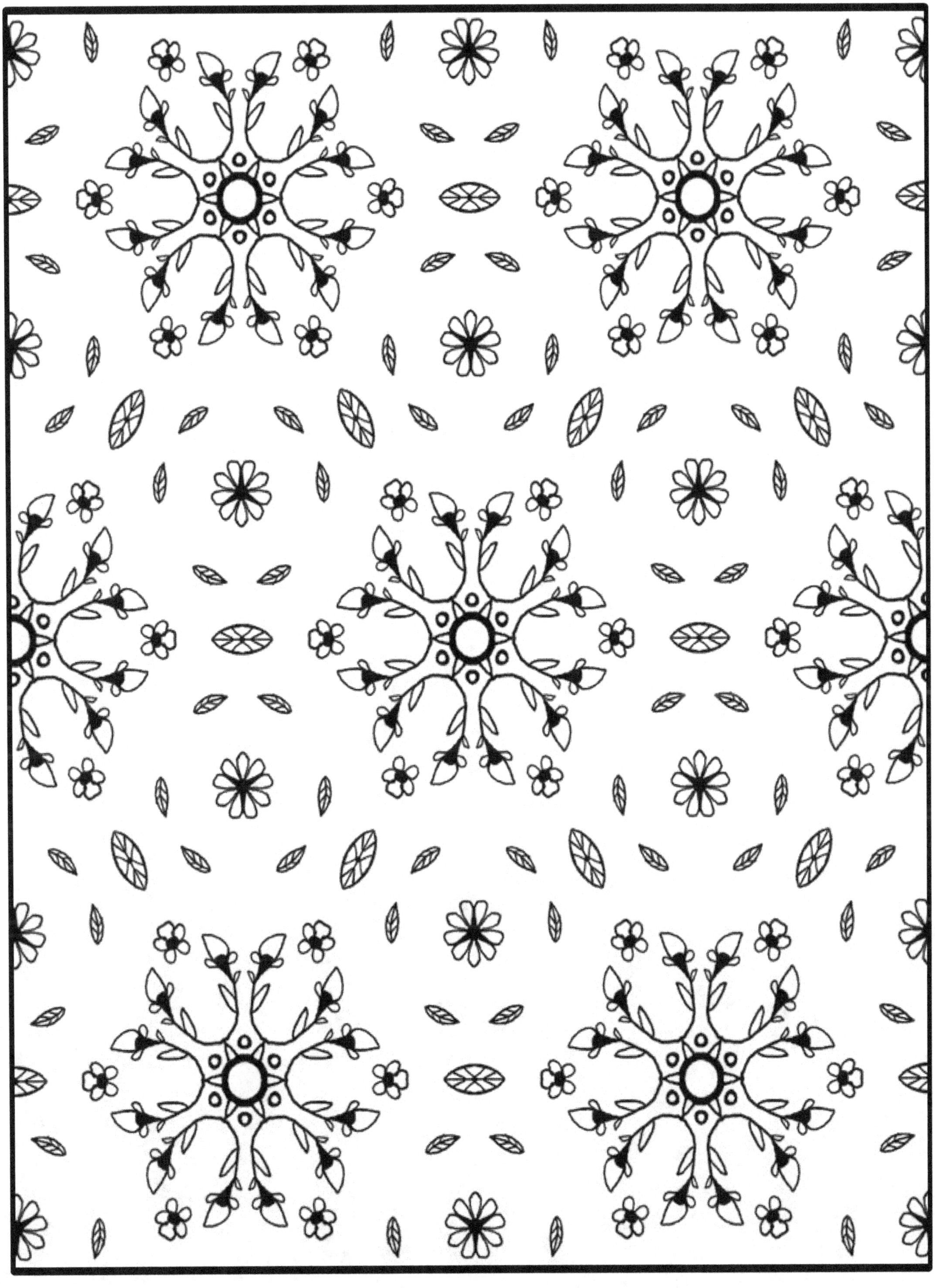

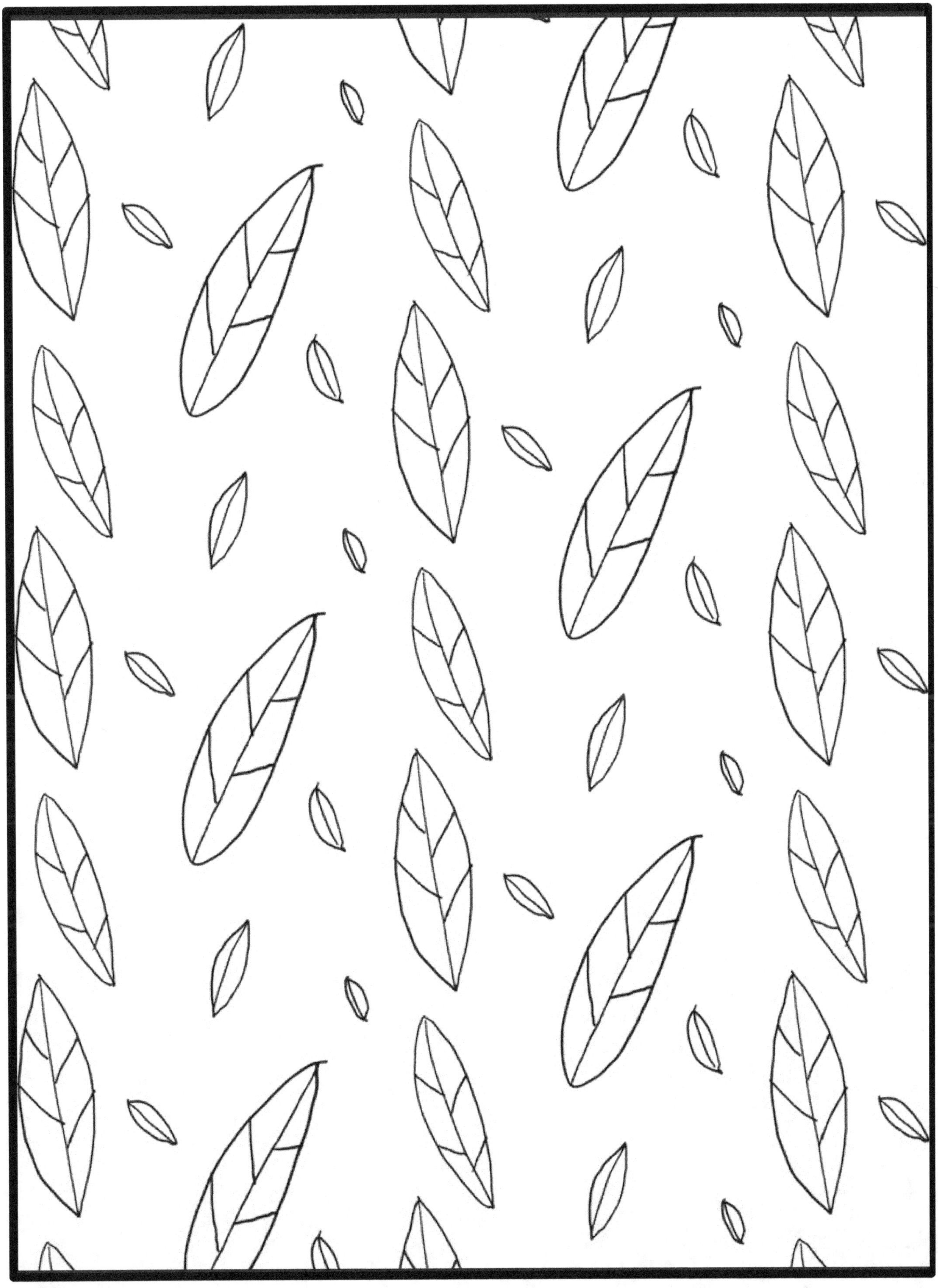

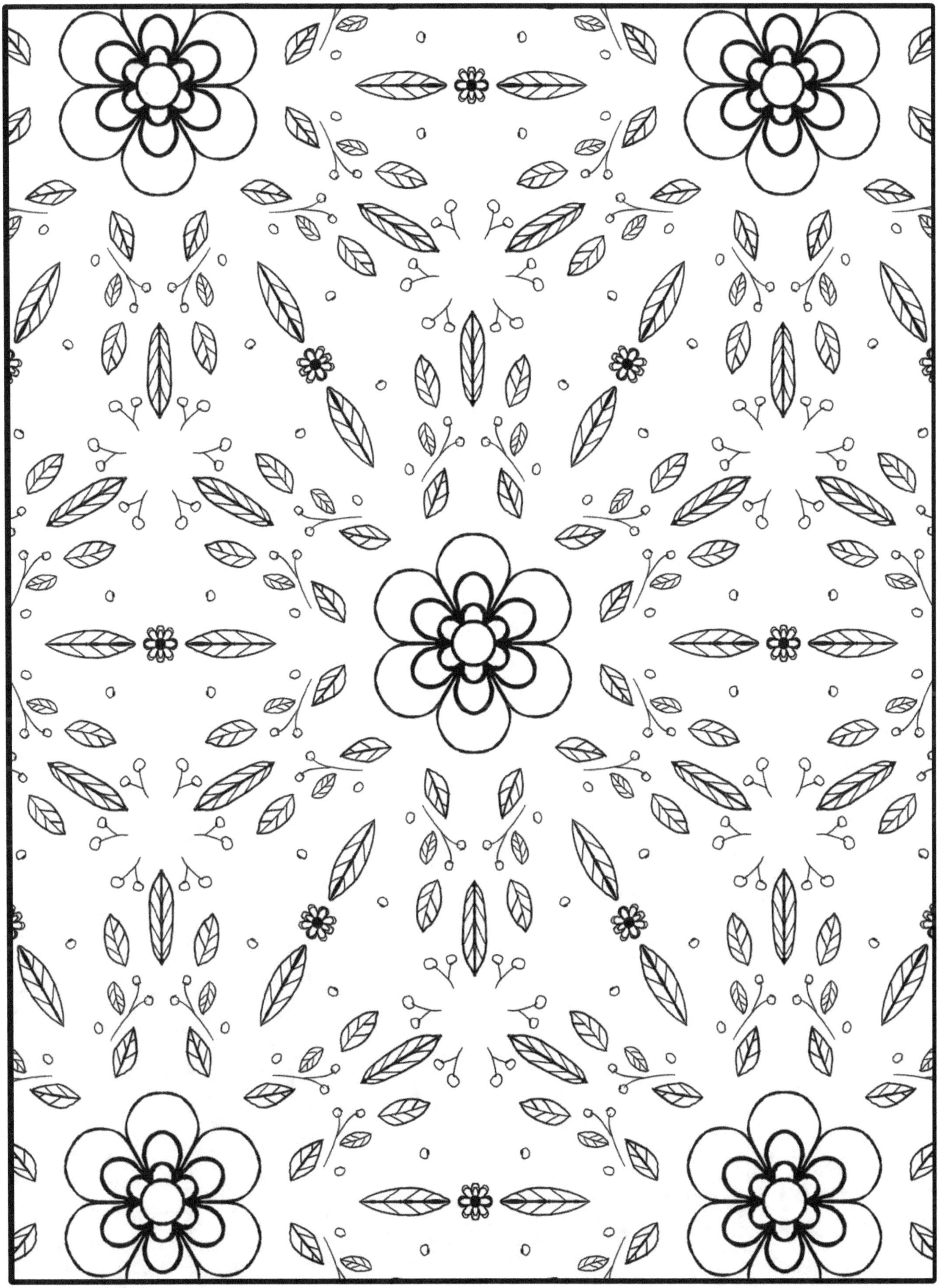

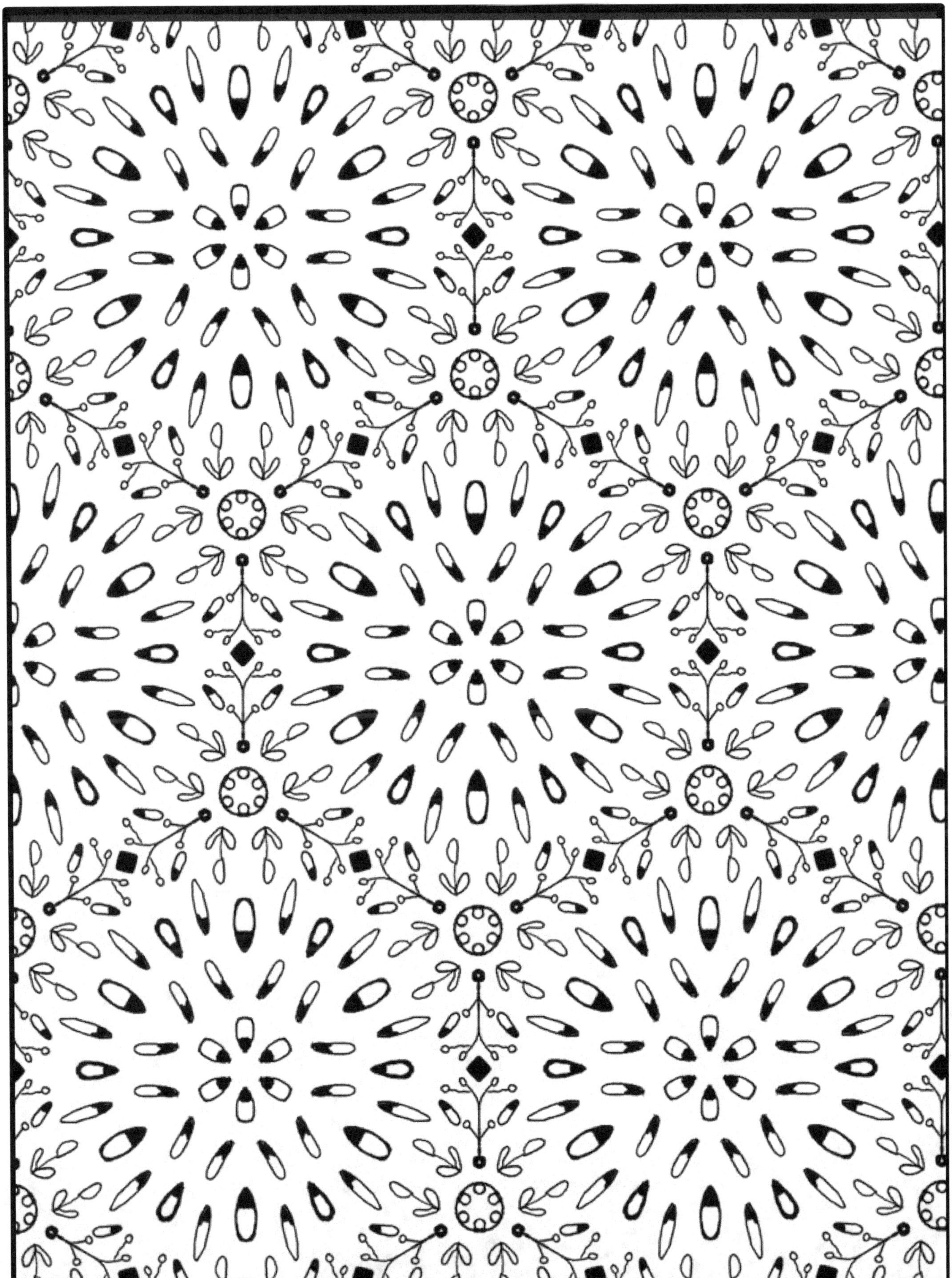

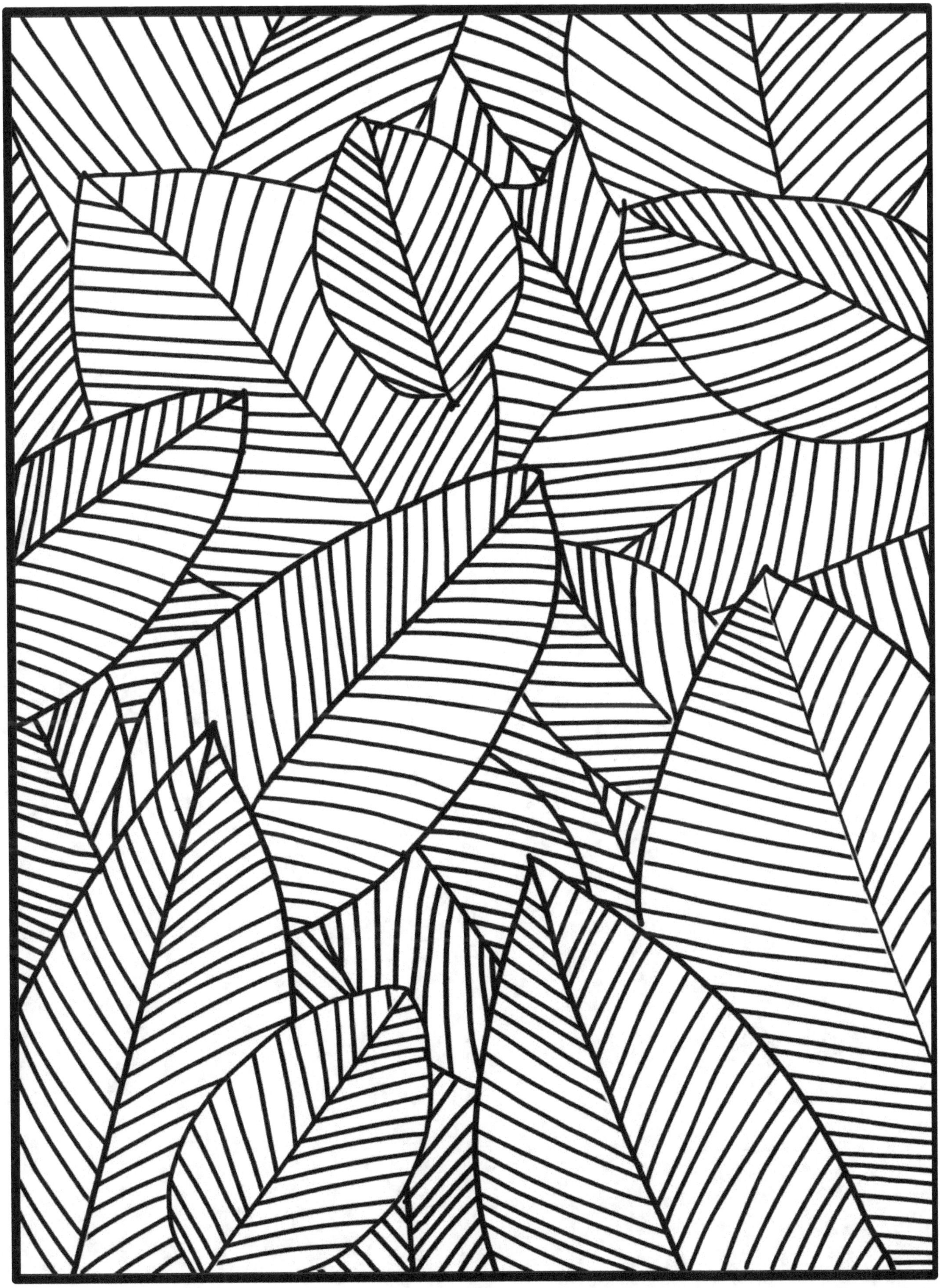

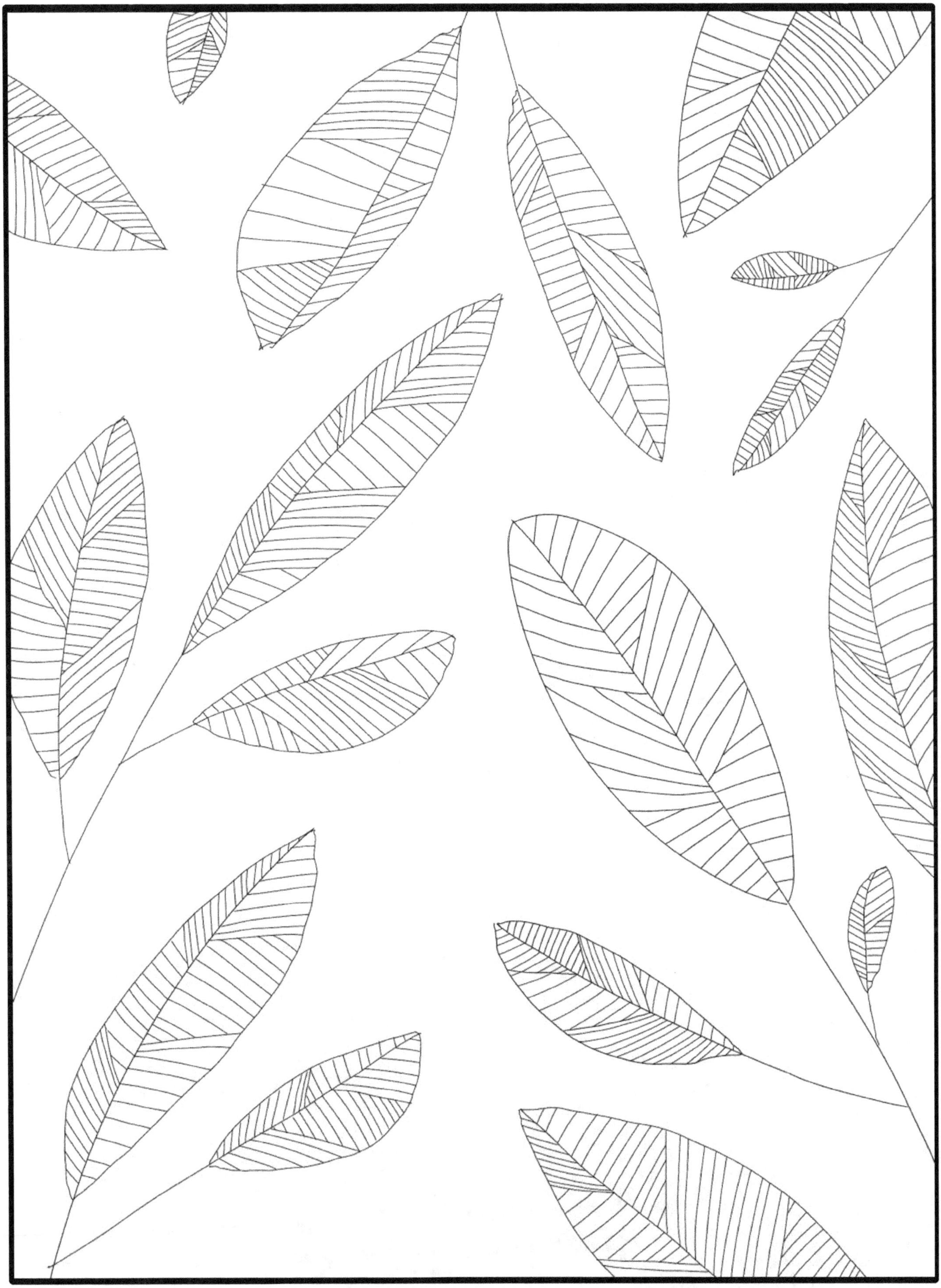

Color Test Page

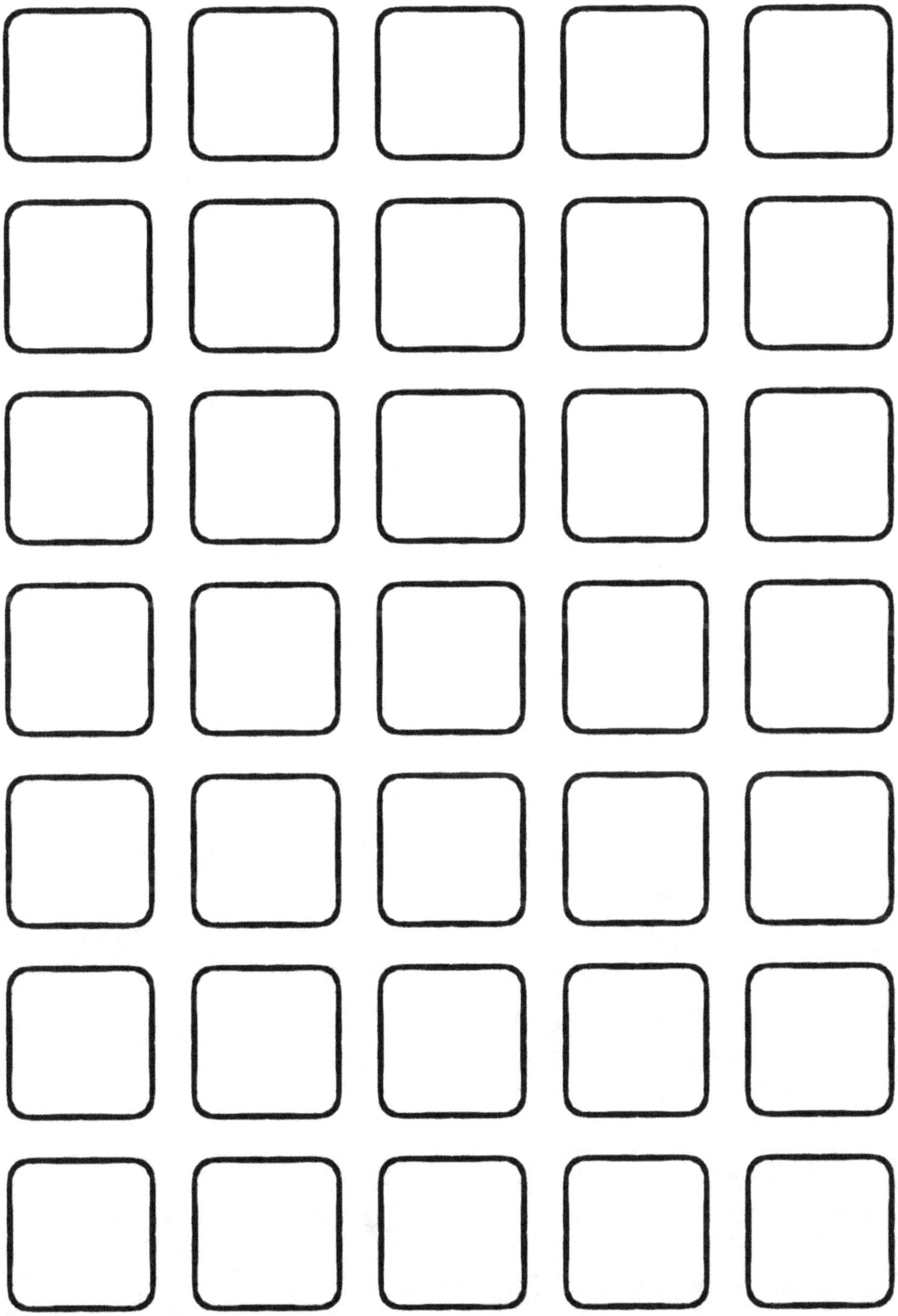

Color Test Page

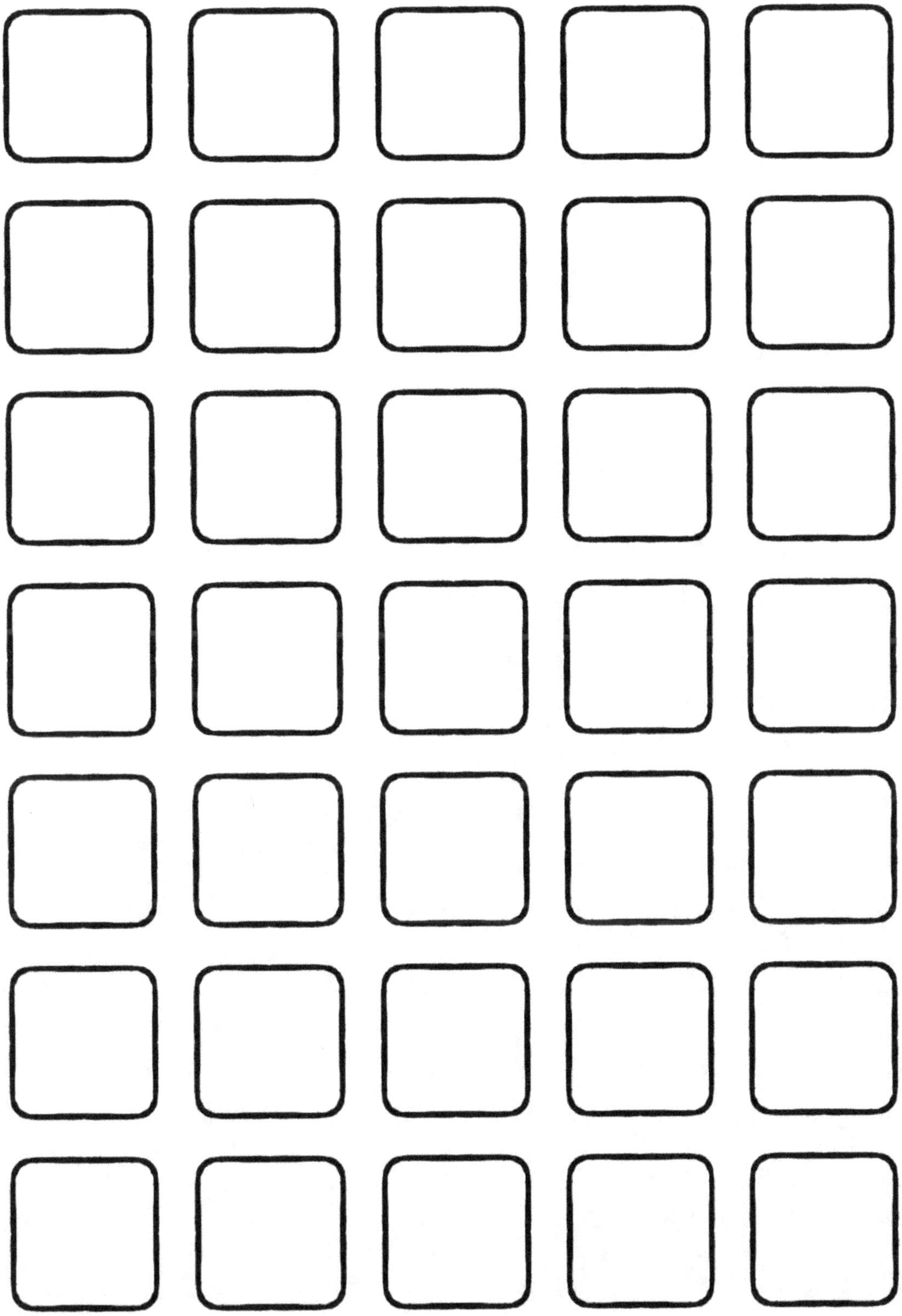

www.ingramcontent.com/pod-product-compliance
Lightning Source LLC
Chambersburg PA
CBHW080510220526
45465CB00006B/2434
* 9 7 9 8 6 6 2 8 2 5 2 5 3 *